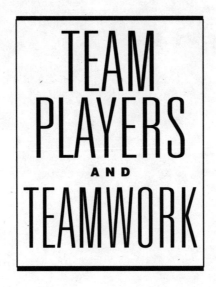

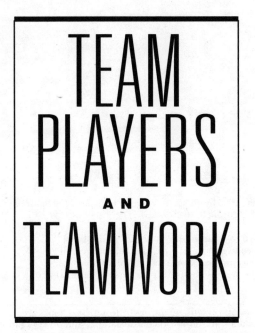

The New Competitive
Business Strategy

Glenn M. Parker

Jossey-Bass Publishers
San Francisco

Substantial discounts on bulk quantities of Jossey-Bass books are available to corporations, professional associations, and other organizations. For details and discount information, contact the special sales department at Jossey-Bass Inc., Publishers. (415) 433-1740; Fax (800) 605-2665.

For sales outside the United States, please contact your local Simon & Schuster International Office.

Manufactured in the United States of America on Lyons Falls Pathfinder Tradebook. This paper is acid-free and 100 percent totally chlorine-free.

Library of Congress Cataloging-in-Publication Data

Parker, Glenn M., date.
   Team players and teamwork : the new competitive business strategy / Glenn M. Parker. — 1st ed.
     p.   cm.—(Jossey-Bass management series)
   Includes bibliographical references and index.
   ISBN 1-55542-257-8 (alk. paper)
   ISBN 0-7879-0185-7 (paperback)
   1. Work groups. 2. Corporate culture. I. Title. II. Series.
HD66.P346   1990
658.4′036—dc20   90-53093

FIRST EDITION
HB Printing   10 9 8 7
PB Printing   10 9 8 7 6 5 4 3 2 1

The Jossey-Bass
Business & Management Series

Contents

The Ineffective Communicator • The Ineffective
Challenger • Dealing with the Ineffective Team
Player When It Is You • Dealing with the Ineffective
Team Player When It Is Someone Else

Resources: Tools for Developing Teams and Team Players

══════════════Preface══════════════

When I wrote *Team Players and Teamwork* some six years ago, we were only beginning to see the emergence of teamwork as an important business strategy. Quality circles had a good run of popularity during the late seventies and early eighties but failed to gain substantial support outside of manufacturing. Even when successful, quality circles were rarely part of an overall corporate strategy.

In the eighties we saw the outline of an emerging movement toward self-directed teams, cross-functional teams, and a total quality management process that was heavily team-based. Since then, reengineering has leaped on to the scene and been embraced with an almost religious zeal. Even more recently, we have witnessed a fascination with something called a "high performing organization." But both of these trends—reengineering and high performing organizations—include teams as part of their core strategy.

My point is that teams are not fading away like so many other management fads because no matter what the organizational goal, teams are integral to success. For example, teams have been at the core of successful organizational efforts to:

- Reduce the time it takes to bring a new product to the market
- Provide quality customer service and speedy turnaround time on customer requests
- Collaborate with business partners around the world
- Reengineer the design of work processes

- Improve the quality of products and services
- Reduce costs and eliminate waste
- Establish an empowered work force
- Increase sales and improve after sales support
- Design and implement an organizational change effort.
- Reduce cross-functional competition and "turf" conflicts
- Devise creative and innovative improvements to business processes, product development, and service delivery systems

In this book I challenge the traditional view of a team. A team is no longer simply a group of people working in the same area, on the same equipment, with the same customers, and with everyone eating in the same cafeteria. Now our teammates may include people outside of the organization, many of whom we see infrequently, such as customers and suppliers, people in other countries, people in other time zones, and people in other cultures. This book helps team leaders and members address this new reality of teams composed of a diverse group of people.

In *Team Players and Teamwork*, I describe in detail what it means to be a team player. In the past, there has been a rather one-dimensional view of a team player as someone who went along and supported the company "program" without question—someone who was often described as a "good soldier." A team player, it was said, lived by the credo that "to get along, you go along." In this book I reject that view and replace it with a much more complex concept of a team player. A team player cannot be described by a single profile or job description. It is my view, supported by research, that there are four types of team players—Contributor, Collaborator, Communicator, and Challenger—each with its own strengths and potential weaknesses. At the time *Team Players and Teamwork* was first published, I did not anticipate how popular this view of team players would become.

Understanding the four team player styles helps team leaders and members better understand themselves and how they contribute to team success. This book's Team Player Survey provides a tool for people to identify their own style and thereby gain insight into their individual strengths as well as a means to develop a plan to increase their effectiveness as team players. The Team Development Survey, which measures team success against twelve benchmark characteristics, is a starting point for team building. (Since the first publication of this book, research has further validated these concepts and resulted in revisions of both surveys. The Team Player Survey and Team Development Survey have both been revised and published in booklet form.[1])

As my work shows, the high performing organizations of the future will place great value on team players. With change the only constant, the successful employees will be the ones who can quickly adjust and work effectively with new and different people. As Tom Peters has pointed out, one organizational model for the future is the movie production crew—a group of people who come together for a brief period of time, work in an intensely collaborative environment, and then deliver a product that is the result of their combined efforts. The successful crew members are able to quickly and easily focus on the goal, share their unique expertise, build relationships with diverse team members, and deliver the goods on schedule. I describe such a person as an *effective team player*.

We are just beginning to see organizations take concrete action reflecting the high value they place on team players. For example, Saturn Corporation recently ran a "help wanted" ad that said in part, "We're not looking for employees. We are looking for a few new team members. People who think for themselves, work creatively, and are willing to take risks. . . . People who are open to change and can listen to other ideas." Saturn and other organizations have realized that one of the best ways to create a team-based environment is to recruit and hire people who are team players.

Organizations are experimenting with their performance management systems as vehicles for encouraging team player behavior. For example, some companies are incorporating peer appraisals into their performance review systems. In other organizations, senior management considers team player behaviors when making decisions about who will be assigned to critical teams, who will lead the key teams, and who will be promoted to important management positions.

[1]Surveys available from Xicom, Sterling Forest, Tuxedo, NY 10987. A video depicting the four team player styles is available from CRM Films, 1801 Avenue of the Stars, Los Angeles, CA 90067.

No matter what the industry, effective teamwork is critical for success. And teamwork starts with team players—individuals working together to accomplish agreed upon goals and objectives. Learn what it takes to become an effective team player in a successful team, and the rewards of better products, quality service, reasonable costs, and higher profits will follow.

Background and Purpose of the Book

Team Players and Teamwork provides specific and practical help for people who want to know how to get more team play in their organizations. For the first time, there is a clear answer to the question "What is a team player?" In fact, that very question was the genesis of this book. It was asked by a manager of a client company in which I was working on ways to improve the performance appraisal system. I pointed out that, although management talked about teamwork throughout the year, it was rarely mentioned during the annual performance appraisal discussions. Somewhat frustrated, one manager asked, "What do we look for? What does a team player really do?" With that question began the journey that culminated in the writing of this book.

The data that form the basis of this book come from a survey of fifty-one companies. Managers and human resource professionals in a variety of industries completed a preliminary open-ended questionnaire. The result of this effort was a structured survey instrument that was mailed to the chief executive officers and vice-presidents of human resources of the one hundred top companies in the 1987 *Fortune* list of America's most admired corporations.

My research indicates that there are many ways in which a person can be a team player, and positive process is just one of them. I have conceptualized these skills and behaviors into four team-player styles that form the heart of *Team Players and Teamwork*. I have expanded the earlier work on teams by showing the many ways team players contribute to effective teamwork. And I have enlarged our understanding of leadership by outlining the specific approaches team players use to carry out key leadership functions. A team player can be both a leader and a member. In fact, during the course of a day, a person may occupy both roles as he or she moves from one team to another. But a person's team-player style will remain relatively constant even though the expectations placed on him or her will change as the role (leader or member) changes.

In the final analysis, this book is both inspirational and prescriptive. Above all, it should convince the reader of the value of team players and the many ways in which team players can benefit an organization. And it will help readers identify and assess team play when the time comes for performance appraisals. In addition, the book includes a guide for organizations that want to move toward a team-player culture.

Audiences

I wrote *Team Players and Teamwork* with practitioners in mind—leaders in the private, public, and nonprofit sectors who are looking for answers. I see the book as a resource guide on teamwork for people who are ready for something more than exhortation or a compilation of group exercises. *Team Players and Teamwork* is for people who see teamwork as a practical business strategy and want to know how to make it come alive in their organizations. I hope the book will convince readers that team players are critical to the success of the team.

This book is designed for a number of different audiences:

• It will be invaluable to business and government leaders who want specific advice on how to change their organizations to increase the quality of teamwork and develop a culture that places a high value on team players. The book includes suggestions drawn from the experience of managers of successful corporations.

• Middle managers and supervisors who want more team players in their organizations and who want to know what to look for in recruitng, evaluating, and promoting employees will find this book valuable. *Team Players and Teamwork* describes the specific behaviors that characterize team players.

• Human resource planners and policy makers who want to change their performance appraisal, succession planning, and managerial assessment programs to emphasize teamwork and team players will find much useful advice here. My detailed descriptions of effective and ineffective team players provide the basis for designing successful human resource assessment and development programs.

• Leaders of business teams, task forces, committees, quality circles, autonomous work groups, new product teams, project teams, and other similar teams will find *Team Players and Teamwork* a practical handbook. Leaders will find especially helpful the discussion of the role of the team player as team leader and the methodology for analyzing the strengths and weaknesses of a specific team.

• Team members who want to become more effective team players and increase the effectiveness of their teams will find this book extremely useful. The many checklists, guidelines, and surveys provide the basis for a personal development effort. In addition, the book offers clear advice on increasing team effectiveness at each stage of team development.

• Developers of training programs will find the book a valuable resource for designing workshops in team effectiveness. The book includes an in-depth analysis of the dimensions of an effective team and the role of the team player.

• Students of organizational behavior and human resource development will find *Team Players and Teamwork* a valuable reference. The book acknowledges past contributions to our understanding of teams and adds an important new dimension: the concept of team players. As the business world adopts a teamwork strategy, students and those who plan careers in management will find useful insights here.

Overview of the Contents

Team Players and Teamwork begins with a description of the many ways team players are contributing to the success of organizations. Chapter One presents the practical, bottom-line results of teamwork across a variety of industries and occupations. I show how effective teamwork leads to increased productivity, more effective use of resources, cost reduction, improved quality, innovation, better customer service, and more rapid commercialization of products.

Chapter Two reviews our historical understanding of teams and concludes that a more comprehensive approach is needed now for a world characterized by change and complexity. I provide an in-depth description of the twelve characteristics of an effective team and the role of a team player in bringing each characteristic to life. I discuss the ineffective team and describe "signs of trouble" that team leaders can use to detect problems within their teams.

In Chapter Three I depict the four team-player styles that form the heart of the book. Using examples from my consulting practice and other examples from my survey of fifty-one companies, I explain how positive teamwork results from effective team players. Each style description is buttressed by checklists of behaviors and adjectives that will help both leaders and members quickly identify their team-player styles.

Chapter Four begins with an assessment of the organizational costs of ineffective team players. I describe and offer examples of the negative features of each of the four team-player styles. The chapter concludes with guidelines for dealing with ineffective team players.

Because team leadership is critical to team success, I devote Chapter Five to team players as team leaders. I detail how each of the four team-player styles carries out five key leadership functions: planning, communication, risk taking, problem solving, and decision making. In each case I describe the consequences of ineffective leadership. I also provide team leaders with guidelines for personal development and ten successful team-building strategies.

Chapter Six focuses on the four stages of team development—forming, storming, norming, and performing—and how team players successfully adapt to each stage. I describe each stage and pinpoint the key concerns of each team-player style. For each stage and style I recommend actions that will help the team grow and develop into a mature, adaptable organization.

Chapter Seven provides team leaders with a methodology for analyzing the strengths and weaknesses of their teams. I discuss the consequences of having too many people with the same team-player style. I also describe the dangers inherent in a team that is missing one of the four styles. Several sample team profiles are presented as a self-study exercise in team assessment.

In Chapter Eight I offer a prescription to organizational leaders who want to develop a culture that encourages teamwork and values team players. Drawing on examples provided by our survey respondents, I describe a variety of methods used by successful organizations. Job assignments, promotional policies, performance appraisal, awards, and team recognition are among the many techniques outlined in this chapter.

The final chapter presents a series of challenges to leaders, managers, human resource professionals, and training specialists who see team players and teamwork as the centerpiece of a new competitive business strategy.

A resources section includes the Team-Development Survey and the Team-Player Survey. The Team-Development Survey helps a team assess its strengths and weaknesses in terms of the twelve characteristics of an effective team. The Team-Player Survey is an instrument that helps an individual identify his or her primary team-player style.

Acknowledgments

Many people help shaped my thinking and, in turn, the contents of this book. In many cases these individuals are not fully aware of their influence.

I continue to be inspired by the work and writings of Warren Bennis, beginning with his wondership little book *The Temporary Society* (1968, with P. Slater). Peter Block provided inspiration on a personal level coupled with just the right amount of humor. My mentor, Neale Clapp, regularly challenges me to seek higher levels of quality and integrity.

Several clients have taken a personal interest in my work. I am especially indebted to Bill Fox of Bell Communications Research (BELLCORE) for his encouragement, honest feedback, and openness to new ideas.

As an independent consultant, I need the friendship and support of colleagues for sustenance. Over the years, I have held various offices, served on many committees, and been involved in several support groups of the American Society of Training and Development (ASTD). People who, at various times, encouraged me, prodded me, cared about me, and made me laugh include Ira Blatt, Stephanie Donato, David Gilman, Maria Grasso, Howard Guttmen, Vic Kline, Dick Kropp, Jerry Middlemiss, and Peg Urda.

My oldest personal friend and professional colleague, Ira Asherman, read several chapters and offered comments, and my office mate, Pete Lunetta, suffered with me through the various stages of the book's development. Dee Baker and Teddi Danberry had the patience to wade through my notes to type the manuscript.

My editor at Jossey-Bass, Bill Hicks, pushed me hard to strengthen the book, and I am indebted to him for that. Dr. Jean Kirnan of Trenton State College designed the ongoing validation studies of the Team-Player Survey. Her professionalism and spirit have made this tedious effort enjoyable and rewarding.

Finally, I want to thank my wife, Judy, and my children, Ellen, Jill, and Michael, for their love and patience throughout this process and my parents, Lillian and Mel, for injecting me with the confidence to complete such an undertaking.

Lawrenceville, New Jersey Glenn M. Parker
October 1995

══════ The Author ══════

Glenn M. Parker has worked full-time in the human resource and organization development field since 1962. He received his B.A. degree (1959) from City College of New York in economics and his M.A. degree (1961) from the University of Illinois in industrial relations, and he has studied for a Ph.D. degree at Cornell University. Parker is past president of the mid New Jersey chapter of the American Society for Training and Development (ASTD) and is a frequent speaker at conferences sponsored by ASTD and *Training* magazine. His company, Glenn M. Parker Associates, in Trenton, New Jersey, offers workshops and consulting services on teamwork and team players using the concepts presented in this book.

Parker has specialized in organization development interventions such as team building, strategic planning, survey-feedback, conflict resolution, and quality circles and in training workshops on team effectiveness, goal setting, and trainer development. His clients have included executives, managers, professionals, and wage employees in major corporations across a variety of industries.

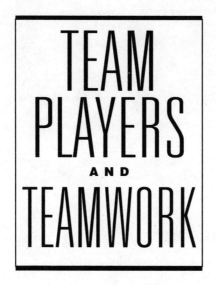

TEAM
PLAYERS
AND
TEAMWORK

Chapter One

Team Players:
The Key to Organizational
Success

Many recent books on business leadership have highlighted the value of teamwork and team players (Kanter, 1983; Peters, 1987; Bradford and Cohen, 1984; Lawler, 1986). In the past, however, team building was pushed more by behavioral scientists than it was accepted and practiced in American business. Teamwork was "nice" but not critical for the success of the corporation. Team building was lumped with other corporate goals that were given more lip service than real backing—goals such as community responsibility, affirmative action, clean environment, and employee development.

Today many of those areas are gaining in importance as public and private sector leaders see the tangible benefits of effective programs. Global competition, work-force changes, the impact of technology, and other factors have pushed organizations in the United States to experiment with team approaches to achieving cost-effective, quality products and services.

Teamwork is paying off with tangible results.

Honeywell's commercial flight division in Minneapolis, devoted largely to manufacturing our navigational systems, switched to team organization about six years ago. Virtually all plant functions, including production, conflict resolution, even allocation of funds, is done by teams. . . . [As a result] Honeywell's Minneapolis plant has 80 percent of the flight-navigational

1

systems market, and 1988 profits were 200 percent above projections [Chance, 1989, p. 18].

GEMICO's [General Electric Mortgage Insurance Company] experience in its Seattle office dramatically illustrates the benefits realized by creating a teamwork mentality. During 1985, GEMICO's market share in Washington hit an all-time low and delinquencies and loan declinations skyrocketed due to deteriorating business quality. At the beginning of 1986, faced with the prospect of withdrawing from the state, GEMICO's branch manager and newly-hired experienced sales representatives began to work together to turn the situation around. First, everyone agreed that their goal would be to increase the volume of quality business received from Washington lenders. Second, everyone on the team demonstrated a willingness to "wear different hats" to see this task accomplished. Sales reps met with lenders to discuss underwriting problems, and supported (rather than second-guessed) underwriters when loans were declined. At the same time, branch office underwriters accompanied sales reps on customer calls, and loan processors served as unofficial customer service reps. The result: GEMICO market share in Washington has more than doubled, while loan declinations have been cut in half and delinquency rates have dropped from 3.05 percent to 2.52 percent, lower than the average for all mortage insurers [Barmore, 1987, p. 94].

At Xerox headquarters in Rochester, New York, on a typical work day they [encoders] process about 6,000 customer payment checks worth about $6 million. With that level of volume, operators were frequently so overwhelmed that checks were left undeposited until the next time, watering down the company's return on assets.

Xerox encourages team problem solving—even awarding those groups that find new ways to cut costs or improve quality—so that's what the encoders did. They formed a team and set to work analyzing the problem.

The encoders found that productivity, morale, and communication were better on Saturdays than any other of the six work days. The reason: work flow was managed through a coordinator Monday through Friday, leaving the encoders little control over what got processed, by whom, or when. On Saturdays, when the encoders had to distribute their work, assign machines, and juggle their lunch breaks themselves, workflow was far better. The end result: The coordinator position was eliminated. Now the encoders form a "huddle" twice daily at mail delivery time to divide the work. In one month, they found a 21 percent reduction in the number of checks carried over to the next business day, a 70 percent decrease in overtime, $7000 in ROA improvements, and immeasurable improvement in employee morale, communication, and employee involvement ["Copy Cats Worth Copying," 1988, p. 28].

Cheesebrough-Ponds used a high-intensity task force to reformulate and reposition its Rave Home Permanent product as Rave Moisturelock Perm. Management organized a team which included the brand group, research and development, packaging and the agency account group [Feder and Mitchell, 1988, p. 21].

Pratt and Whitney used special teams to reinvigorate its production capability by reconfiguring its engine manufacturing operations into numerous small units [Herman and Herman, 1989, p. 90].

Keithley Instruments' plant in Salem, Ohio, saw output increase by 90 percent and absenteeism fall by 75 percent when its production teams went to work [Chance, 1989, p. 18].

A five-part management plan provided the framework for management improvement in the Department of Agriculture. Much of the credit goes to an emphasis on innovation and the cooperative effort of many employees [Franke, 1988–89, p. 11].

A recent study reported schools that have team management outperform schools that have hierarchical management (Chubb, 1988).

For example, many school districts in Marin County, California, are encouraging a team-based effort which, among other things, schedules time for teachers and staff to work together and share decision making at all levels (Lambert, 1989).

Teamwork has also proven to be a powerful tool for reducing racism. In the 1970s, several research projects demonstrated that the least prejudiced students were those who had participated in sports teams and school bands with members of other races. Recently, experiments with interracial learning teams have led to a reduction in prejudice among students in the United States, Israel, and Canada. Team members learn together and are encouraged to help each other. Although they are tested individually, the team also gets a score or other forms of recognition (Coleman, 1989). This approach may have important implications for smoothing the transitions associated with corporate mergers and for dealing with the expanding cultural diversity of the work force.

In other areas, management, workers, and, often, unions are teaming up to regain and maintain the competitive edge. Quality circles have passed through the fad stage and are now used as a strategy for changing the cultures at many companies and government agencies. Fundamentally, the quality-circle approach is a team-based strategy for improving quality and reducing costs. On the heels of quality circles came the total-quality approach ("do it right the first time") advocated by Philip Crosby (1979) and implemented at scores of companies across the country. One of the most dramatic efforts to meet the global challenge has been the cooperation of Japanese and American auto manufacturers and U.S. trade unionists. The New United Motor Manufacturing Inc. (NUMMI) joint venture of Toyota and General Motors, with the United Automobile Workers as the bargaining agent, is the most famous example. "In just four years, it has achieved productivity and quality levels that exceed anything in the American auto industry, and which rival Japan's best" (Lee, 1988).

Many other automobile companies are following the Japanese lead and implementing team production. For example, at the new Mazda Motor Manufacturing (USA) plant in Flat Rock, Michigan, the team method means "Workers learn several jobs and are expected to participate in problem-solving" (Kertesz, 1988, p. 36).

Another team experiment being closely watched by American automakers is the new Volvo plant in Uddevalla, Sweden. Volvo has traded the traditional assembly line for self-managed work teams of seven to ten employees. "Each team works in one area and assembles four cars per shift. Since members are trained to handle all assembly jobs, they work an average of three hours before repeating the same task" (Kapstein and Hoerr, 1989, p. 92).

Change as the Norm

Change is the norm in American business today. The lexicon of corporate America is replete with the words and phrases of transformation:

Acquisition	Downsizing
Merger	Restructuring
Takeover	Rationalization
Buyout	Outplacement
Diversification	Reintegration

With organizational change comes the need for adaptive people who can work with a diverse group on an acquisition team (Epstein, 1989), move rapidly into new situations, and create transition task forces and effective new business teams. They know what it takes to be an effective team player. Joseph L. Dionne, chairman and chief executive officer (CEO) of McGraw-Hill Inc., believes strongly that teamwork and team players are important keys to a smooth and successful acquisition process (Dionne, 1988).

An outgrowth of both the loss of America's worldwide competitive edge and the institutionalization of change has been the new "lean and mean" look of American business. Everywhere there is talk of head-count restrictions, budget cuts, eliminating the fat, cutting overhead, and using temporary help. In this era, teamwork and team players are critical to success. As the number of people decreases while the volume of work and the standards remain the same, organizations will need people who do quality work the first time, pitch in to help others out, quickly create a cooperative atmosphere, and challenge others to do the best job possible.

As Jamieson and O'Mara (forthcoming) have shown, the work force is changing dramatically with important implications for teamwork. The work force of the future will simply be more diverse in terms of age, sex, education, cultural background, disabilities, and values. The teamwork implications are significant. The values of this work force in terms of the desire for self-management, information, and involvement point to teams as a way of organizing work. The increasing cultural diversity of the employee group demands one of the important skills of a team player—the ability to work with people who are different. While the education level is increasing, so is the rate of functional illiteracy. Couple this with an economy that is demanding more brain than brawn from its workers and you have a serious problem. At the same time, "Many formerly fragmented tasks are being converted into jobs requiring multiple skills. Computer networks, integrating diverse functions, also require employees who can work as a team" (Pennar and Mandel, 1989, p. 158). Motorola, Ford, Xerox, Polaroid, and Eastman Kodak are among a small but growing number of companies that are heavily committed to providing training in basic reading and arithmetic skills along with team-player skills (Berger, 1989).

One hallmark of a team player is flexibility—the ability and willingness to pitch in and do what is necessary to get the job done. One way to facilitate flexibility is cross-training. Many companies are finding that training employees in several skills while eliminating a long list of narrowly defined job classifications is helping them respond faster to the market, thereby increasing efficiency, quality, productivity, and job satisfaction (Alster, 1989). For example, a team of multiskilled workers at General Motors cut warranty costs on rear-wheel-drive suspension systems by 400 percent in two years. At Corning's Blackburg, Virginia, plant, where they produce ceramic components that are sold to submanufacturers for catalytic converters, a flexible production process was the key to success. Since customers purchased parts of their own individual designs in small quantities, the plant was set up to switch quickly from one model to another. Corning opted for self-managing work teams composed of cross-trained employees able to move easily from one job to another.

Complexity as the Norm

The sheer complexity of business today means that no one person can know it all. With the widening of the marketplace, the increasing importance of technology, the imperative of innovation, and the new focus on the customer, teams, especially cross-functional groups, are becoming the only way to develop viable business solutions. People will be required to work with many other people whose backgrounds and styles may be quite different. Engineers no longer will work on project teams just with other engineers. Now they will work on task forces with people from information systems, operations, purchasing, marketing, finance, and human resources. The challenge to build effective teams composed of effective team players is upon us. The benefits of having teams composed of effective team players are impressive, and reports of new and unusual collaborative efforts are just now coming in.

The traditionally antagonistic relationship between design engineers and buyers in the purchasing department is now a model of teamwork in an increasing number of companies. For example, at Easco Hand Tools in Hunt Valley, Maryland, a new product team "typically includes marketing, engineering, purchasing, manufacturing, quality assurance and suppliers. Marketing can provide direction on what the customer wants, while others address issues such as manufacturability and cost-effectiveness—with engineering handling the technical side of vendor dealings and purchasing handling the commercial side" (Dowst and Raia, 1988, p. 81).

The sales and credit departments, which historically have had divergent goals, are now seeing the profitability of cross-functional teamwork. Team players in sales are seeing the unprofitability of a customer who fails to pay, and credit team players are recognizing that sales on credit must involve some degree of risk (Merchant, 1987). Team players inform the salesperson about credit problems with a customer. And effective sales team players can be helpful in resolving credit problems because they usually have closer relationships with the customers.

In the North American automobile industry, where cooperation among management, employees, and unions is becoming more commonplace, a new player is being added to the team—the sup-

plier. A report by Arthur Anderson and Company stressed a need
to build teamwork among manufacturers, unions, and suppliers as
a basis for maintaining the competitive edge (Versical, 1987).

The supermarket industry, once a bastion of autocratic management, is moving toward visionary leadership and participative management styles (Weinstein, 1987). Corporate leaders at Super Valu
Stores, Lucky Stores, Associated Wholesale Grocers, and Super
Food Services are pushing involvement as a strategy for more effective business decisions. Former professional basketball player Jack
Twyman, now chairman of Super Foods Services in Dayton, Ohio,
is especially supportive of the need for team players.

Some other strange teammates are emerging as manufacturers are
teaming up with distributors and, in the process, are locking out
competitors (Moore, 1989). Mortgage bankers are targeting the real
estate agent rather than the buyer as the customer. Citicorp, for
example, offers fast turnaround on loan applications as an incentive
to agents to refer buyers to the bank. Major airlines have identified
the travel agent, not the passenger, as the client and are using com-
puterized reservation systems that favor their airline.

In the highly individualistic mortgage banking industry, many
companies are turning to a team approach "where loan originators,
processors, underwriters, closers, shippers and management are all
working together as a collective group toward a common goal"
(Evans and Baker, 1987, p. 40).

Our survey of fifty-one companies revealed that the three top
benefits of team players were better problem solving, greater productivity, and effective use of resources. The survey results are summarized in Table 1. All three of those benefits are so interrelated that
it is possible to treat them as a group. When asked to discuss and
give an example of the value of team players to the organization,
a telecommunications company manager in our survey group said
it pointedly: "Network architecture planning is so broad a field that
no one person can do it alone. We must use a team approach and
people must be team players."

Productivity, Use of Resources, and Problem Solving

Minnesota Mining and Manufacturing (3M), a company that bets
its future on creativity and innovation, put greater productivity,

**Table 1. Rank Order of How Companies Benefit
from People Being Team Players.**

Benefits	Rank
Greater productivity	1
Effective use of resources	1
Better problem solving	1
Better quality products and services	2
Creativity and innovation	3
Higher-quality decisions	3

problem solving, resource utilization, and creativity at the top of its team-player benefit list. In responding to our survey, chairman and CEO A. F. Jacobson said that team players were directly responsible for "engineering, installing and shaking down a new process in an Italian factory that produced on time, below cost and high quality performance."

At a very different company in our survey, Cummins Engine, in Columbus, Indiana, team players produce benefits such as "higher production, less cost, better quality and on-time delivery of product." In a story designed to illustrate the point, a bottleneck in a process was eliminated by data collection, by focusing on the problem with no finger pointing, and by team players working together to develop solutions based on the data. Later, data showed a marked improvement in cost and quality of the product.

In another industry, an executive at Anheuser-Busch reported that effective team players increase the effective use of corporate resources. "There is less redundancy and reduced energy wasted on organizational politics." In a similar view expressed in our survey, Howard Guttman of Johnson & Johnson's Personal Products Company has seen organizational benefit from people being team players because "When individuals function as team players the level of trust increases between members. As a result there is a greater likelihood of issues being raised and dealt with, more cooperation versus competition and greater productivity—principally because energy is expanded towards the task as opposed to nonproductive political maneuvering."

Many companies are making effective use of resources through team techniques in systems development. "During group sessions, nontechnical end users and information systems staff meet on a common ground to hammer out systems solutions that truly meet the needs of everyone—especially the needs of end-user management" (Leavitt, 1987, p. 78). Cigna Company in Philadelphia, CNA Insurance Company in Chicago, Ford Motor Company in Dearborn, Michigan, and Chase Manhattan Bank in New York are all using group design techniques to ensure that system requirements are on target. All of the group methodologies require effective goal setting, listening, facilitation skills, consensus building, and a willingness to communicate in ways that can be understood by people with different types of skills and expertise. "Application Engineering" is another cross-functional team approach that ensures the information systems plan is in line with the overall business plan (Goslin, 1988). These team techniques in systems development make effective use of resources, but they also result in measurable benefits. Travelers Corporation, an insurance company based in Hartford, Connecticut, reports that a three-day group design session saved two to three months in analysis time (Kull, 1987).

Quality Products and Services

Quality and customer service are emerging as key points on the agenda of most businesses. Review the corporate credo or vision statement of just about any organization today and you will find quality and service as number one or number two on the list. Therefore, it is not surprising that the respondents in our survey ranked "quality products and services" as one of the most important benefits of team players.

Examples abound, and most of them come from cross-functional teams. It seems clear that the wave of the future in teamwork is in teams composed of people from different work areas. Although these teams are the most difficult to build, the payoffs are potentially greater than from teams in a single work area.

At Pacific Telesis, Mark Hickey, director of human resources policy, points to the "joint efforts of sales and provisioning within Pacific Bell organizing around customers to bring quality products and services closer to them."

Sometimes team-player behavior goes counter to the corporate culture. If the organizational norm is "do your own thing," then working together may not be valued and certainly not recognized and rewarded. In these cases, the initial thrust toward team playing takes a leader—someone who will champion the cause. In his response to our survey, G. B. Vernon, vice-president of Conagra, Inc., gave this example:

> We are a very decentralized company. However, a member of one operating division saw a corporate-wide selling opportunity, pulled together executives from seven of our other businesses, developed a "corporate sale" concept which led to one of the largest single sales and one of the strongest customer relationships we have.

In many industries, most notably consumer packaged goods and pharmaceuticals, new-product development is the single most critical element in maintaining the competitive edge. Product development teams now include a diverse group of players from research, marketing, planning, operations, finance, and regulatory, among others. Underpinning this diversity concept is the belief, based upon empirical evidence, that these teams produce higher-quality products in record time. The competitive edge requires rapid response to customer needs and the ability to be first to the market with new products.

As we go forward into the 1990s, speed will be a critical factor in the product development process. And strange as it may seem, the team approach is emerging as a strategy for reducing the product development time frame. Not too long ago, many people would have agreed with the cynic's definition of a committee as "a group of people who take minutes and waste hours." Now, however, teams operating in a culture amenable to rule bending are able to cut development time by up to 50 percent in some cases.

The key tactic is the multidisciplinary team composed of team players from various departments throughout the company. The telecommunications giant AT&T used to have a cumbersome two-year process to develop a new telephone. Players stayed in their areas until they received handoffs from the previous department. In an effort to speed up the process, John Hanley, an AT&T vice-president of product development, "formed teams of six to 12, including engineers, manufacturers, and marketers, with authority to make every decision on how the product would work, look, be made and cost. The key was to set rigid speed requirements—six weeks, say, for freezing all design specs. Because the team didn't need to send each decision up the line for approval, it could meet these strict deadlines. With this new approach, AT&T cut development time for the 2400 phone from two years to just a year while lowering costs and increasing quality" (Dumaine, 1989a, p. 57).

At Calgon, a team composed of people from research and development, sales, marketing, and manufacturing cut the time it takes to develop a new polymer from twelve to four months (Wolff, 1988). In this case, the team-player mentality was buttressed by a willingness to bend the rules and by extensive customer involvement. The key team-player characteristic was a problem-solving posture with no finger pointing.

A task force representing seven different departments was successful in reducing by one-half the time it takes to introduce a new beer at Adolph Coors Company (Wolff, 1988). The product was Winterfest, a new seasonal beer, which went from concept to market in under a year.

Faced with the twin pressures of more specific customer demands and the prospect of missed opportunities, Honeywell's building controls division went to the team approach for product development. As a result, "The division cut the time from 'concept to carton' by 50–60 percent. In addition, the number of hours devoted to specific projects was reduced by 5 to 10 percent. Improved communications among team members has resulted in fewer changes to new product specifications; this has eliminated much of the rework that lengthens product development cycles" (Larson, 1988).

Procter & Gamble has introduced the concept of category managers to oversee an entire product line. Category managers are using cross-functional teams to speed the launch of new products or the repositioning of old ones. A category manager in conjunction with another new position, the product supply manager, is able to form teams representing sales, financial, and every aspect of manufacturing. "This spring, for example, the category manager for dishwashing detergent wanted a new cap for liquid Cascade. Though the cap was childproof, it was also somewhat adultproof. The team got together . . . to work out all the cost, design and manufacturing problems. The cap went into production without any glitches after only nine months, nearly twice as fast as under the old system" (Dumaine, 1989b, p. 46).

Creativity and Innovation

Ranking third as a benefit of team players in the organization was "creativity and innovation." The old ideas of "two heads are better than one" and, as Linus Pauling is reported to have said, "The best way to get a good idea is to have lots of ideas" are applicable here. Innovation developed out of the efforts of team players is what sets some companies apart from others.

Responding to our survey, Vincent Sarni, chairman of the board of PPG Industries, sent along a copy of the *PPG News,* which was running a series on new product and process researchers. The story featured Samuel Porter, a senior scientist, who is involved in developing and formulating new automotive topcoats. In the story Porter says,

I hope I've made some contributions but really the only way we were able to make advances can be summed up in one word—teamwork. Many of the ideas for work come from the marketing people. They know what the customer needs. We can make a nice, durable coating but if it can't be sold or isn't really what the customer wants, then we've done a lot of work, got a couple of patents and didn't accomplish much for PPG.

There's not one automotive topcoat finish that ever came out of research ready to go. If an idea we develop has a good shot at getting to market, it's the people at the Cleveland Coatings technical lab who get it ready for the customer. They find out whether it can be made in the thousands-of-gallon quantities rather than in five-liter lab flasks. And they test whether or not it will fit into a customer's operations.

Creativity comes in a variety of forms and operates at many levels in an organization. It may not mean a major new product breakthrough, but team players working effectively can create solutions to important problems. For example, at International Flavors and Fragrances, an increase in the yields of the reaction department came as a result of team players conducting a major survey requiring extensive sharing of data involving all three shifts over a long period of time.

At IBM, team-player creativity led to better use of Information Systems (IS). Managers of departments dependent on IS created a task force that developed a workable solution but also saved the company "a significant sum."

Chrysler's cars of the 1990s will be more appealing to the affluent customer due to design innovations resulting from a reorganization of engineers into project teams. These teams, in consultation with marketers and planners, will work on a specific model from inception to production. This team organization differs radically from the old functional approach whereby a group of engineers designed a part for all models. Team-player behavior will be required as everyone responsible for a model will need to work together.

Companies also apply team creativity to their internal management procedures because team players can develop better ways to operate the business. As an example, D. H. Van Lenten, a vice-president at Bell Atlantic, reported that team players had a key role in the complete restructuring of the company. Steering committees were set up to achieve consensus on the complex issues of reporting relationships, staff centralization, force reductions, and many other areas.

In the final analysis, the results are clear. Real team players—not yes-men and yes-women—offer tangible benefits to the company where it counts. Productivity, quality, service, problem solving, innovation, and rapid response are some of the most significant benefits team players bring to a company. They are helping to develop and maintain the competitive edge.

And dare we say it? Being part of an effective team is enjoyable. When asked to report on their most enjoyable work experiences, most people will mention a business team, task force, committee, or other successful team activity. Being an effective team player and working with other effective team players is a great source of personal satisfaction.

It should also be noted that teams can experience times of great frustration due to lack of accomplishment. The next chapter provides guidelines for minimizing the frustration and increasing the opportunities for success.

Chapter Two

What Makes a Team Effective or Ineffective

Teams are everywhere. In business we have new product teams, quality teams, and project teams. In sports we have offensive teams, defensive teams, first teams, second teams, special teams, and all-star teams. In the arts a team is referred to in a variety of ways, including cast, crew, ensemble, company, and troupe. In politics we have party, caucus, coalition, committee, and council.

Teams have an important place in our professional and personal lives. But not every group is a team and not every team is effective. In fact, one of our great frustrations is the failure of teams to function smoothly. This can be seen in comments such as "We need to act more like a team," "The only way we can succeed is to work more like a team," and "We need more team players."

A group of people is not a team. A team is a group of people with a high degree of interdependence geared toward the achievement of a goal or completion of a task. In other words, they agree on a goal and agree that the only way to achieve the goal is to work together.

Bill Fox, division manager at Bell Communications Research, amplifies this definition with a good sports analogy. "The 10,000 runners in the New York City marathon race have a common goal or purpose. However, they are not a team. They are, in fact, in competition with each other. Teamwork requires interdependence—the working together of a group of people with a shared objective. More specifically, the only way the runners can reach their goal is by competitive efforts."

16

Using another track example, Fox argues that a relay team is a good example of a real team. Each member of the team shares a common goal and they must work together to achieve it. All members of an 800-meter relay team must do their part by running fast, passing the baton skillfully, and encouraging each other. While one person could win the 800-meter distance, a team of four people each responsible for 200 meters will win most of the time. The potential for teamwork exists in the relay team. However, success will be dependent upon the degree to which they behave like an effective team.

Teamwork: Lessons from the Past

Our approach to the dimensions of an effective team grows out of and builds on a base of theory and research in behavioral science. While we owe a debt to a few seminal thinkers in organization development, our approach is more comprehensive and responsive to the notion of teamwork as an important business strategy for the 1990s and beyond.

Called the founder of the human relations movement in the United States, Elton Mayo uncovered the importance of teams and the power of the informal system in the workplace. Mayo's most famous research project was conducted at the Hawthorne works of Western Electric Company in Chicago. A preliminary study of the effects of work area lighting on productivity produced some interesting results. Two groups were studied; in one the lighting was varied while in the other the lighting remained constant. The result—in both groups production increased:

At this point the Industrial Research team directed by Mayo took over. The first stage of their inquiry is known as the Relay Assembly Test Room. Six female operatives, engaged in assembling telephone relays, were segregated in order to observe the effect on output and morale of various changes in the conditions of work. During the five years of experiment, various changes were introduced and a continuous record of output was kept. At first a special group payment scheme was introduced: previously the women had been grouped with one hundred other operatives for incentive payment purposes. Other changes introduced at various times were rest pauses in several different forms (varying in length and spacing), shorter hours, and refreshments, in all more than ten changes. Before putting the changes into effect, the investigators spent a lot of time discussing them with the women. Communication between the workers and the research team was very full and open throughout the experimental period. Almost without exception, output increased with each change made [Pugh and Hickson, 1989, p. 173].

It became clear that the six employees in the experimental group had become what we would call a team. They had a clear goal, an informal system of communication and participation, an informal climate, and established decision-making procedures. Communication between the employees and the researchers was also effective. The employee group began to take on many of the characteristics we now associate with effective teams.

In another part of the Hawthorne study, Mayo and his colleagues simply observed a work group without making any changes. They found that the informal system could also produce negative norms. In this case, the group set a standard for individual production and peer pressure enforced the standard. The net result was restricted output. This group had become an ineffective team.

Mayo concluded that it was a major responsibility of management to foster the conditions that promote effective teams. The informal system that Mayo identified persists today as an organizational issue under the rubric of "culture." However, the issues and the teams today are broader and more complex than those studied by Mayo and his colleagues.

During the 1930s, Kurt Lewin focused attention on the behavior of groups and on the forces that help to explain the actions of groups. Lewin's work led to the development of a field of study known as *group dynamics*. His unique contribution was called *force field analysis,* and it helped us understand what people can do to increase the effectiveness of teams (Lewin, 1951).

In Lewin's view, a team is an open social system with a series of forces or vectors applied to it from two sides. If the forces are equal, the team will remain in a state of equilibrium—it will not change. However, if the forces on one side increase or decrease, the balance point will change. For example, if we wanted to change an ineffective team, such as the one that was restricting output in the Hawthorne study, we would devise a plan to reduce or eliminate the forces supporting the negative production norms. Lewin called this *unfreezing*, the first step in the change process. The next step, *moving*, involves the establishment of new norms, values, and behaviors. The final step, *refreezing*, results in a new point of equilibrium where supports exist for the new behavior. Force field analysis is still used today as a technique for improving the effectiveness of teams.

About twenty years later, Douglas McGregor and his colleagues began studying the development of managers in industry. The study culminated in the publication of *The Human Side of Enterprise* (McGregor, 1960), one of the most important books of our time. Most of the book is devoted to an explanation of a set of assumptions about motivation that McGregor labeled *Theory X* and *Theory Y*. However, in the last chapter, McGregor presented a list of the characteristics of effective and ineffective management teams. These lists have had almost as much influence as Theory X and Theory Y.

The Effective Team

1. The "atmosphere" which can be sensed in a few minutes of observation, tends to be informal, comfortable, relaxed. There are no obvious tensions. It is a working atmosphere in which people are involved and interested. There are no signs of boredom.
2. There is a lot of discussion in which virtually everyone participates, but it remains pertinent to the task of the group. If the discussion gets off the subject, someone will bring it back in short order.
3. The task or the objective of the group is well understood and accepted by the members. There will have been free discussion of the objective at some point until it was

formulated in such a way that the members of the group could commit themselves to it.

4. The members listen to each other! The discussion does not have the quality of jumping from one idea to another unrelated one. Every idea is given a hearing. People do not appear to be afraid of being foolish by putting forth a creative thought even if it seems fairly extreme.

5. There is disagreement. The group is comfortable with this and shows no signs of having to avoid conflict or to keep everything on a plane of sweetness and light. Disagreements are not suppressed or overridden by premature group action. The reasons are carefully examined, and the group seeks to resolve them rather than to dominate the dissenter. On the other hand, there is no "tyranny of the minority." Individuals who disagree do not appear to be trying to dominate the group or to express hostility. Their disagreement is an expression of a genuine difference of opinion, and they expect a hearing in order that a solution may be found.

    Sometimes there are basic disagreements which cannot be resolved. The group finds it possible to live with them, accepting them but not permitting them to block its efforts. Under some conditions, action will be deferred to permit further study of an issue between the members. On other occasions, where the disagreement cannot be resolved and action is necessary, it will be taken but with open caution and recognition that the action may be subject to later reconsideration.

6. Most decisions are reached by a kind of consensus in which it is clear that everybody is in general agreement and willing to go along. However, there is little tendency for individuals who oppose the action to keep their opposition private and thus let an apparent consensus mask real disagreement. Formal voting is at a minimum; the group does not accept a simple majority as a proper basis for action.

7. Criticism is frequent, frank, and relatively comfortable.

There is little evidence of personal attack, either openly or in a hidden fashion. The criticism has a constructive flavor in that it is oriented toward removing an obstacle that faces the group and prevents it from getting the job done.

8.   People are free in expressing their feelings as well as their ideas both on the problem and on the group's operation. There is little pussyfooting, there are few "hidden agendas." Everybody appears to know quite well how everybody else feels about any matter under discussion.

9.   When action is taken, clear assignments are made and accepted.

10.   The chairman of the group does not dominate it, nor on contrary, does the group defer unduly to him. In fact, as one observes the activity, it is clear that the leadership shifts from time to time, depending on the circumstances. Different members, because of their knowledge or experience, are in a position at various times to act as "resources" for the group. The members utilize them in this fashion and they occupy leadership roles while they are thus being used. There is little evidence of a struggle for power as the group operates. The issue is not who controls but how to get the job done.

11.   The group is self-conscious about its own operations. Frequently, it will stop to examine how well it is doing or what may be interfering with its operation. The problem may be a matter of procedure, or it may be an individual whose behavior is interfering with the accomplishment of the group's objectives. Whatever it is, it gets open discussion until a solution is found.

The Ineffective Team

1.   The "atmosphere" is likely to reflect either indifference and boredom (people whispering to each other or carrying on side conversations, individuals who are obviously not involved, etc.) or tension (undercurrents of hostility and antagonism, stiffness and undue formality, etc.).

The group is clearly not challenged by its task or genuinely involved in it.

2. A few people tend to dominate the discussion. Often
    their contributions are way off the point. Little is done
    by anyone to keep the group clearly on the track.

3. From the things which are said, it is difficult to under-
    stand what the group task is or what its objectives are.
    These may have been stated by the chairman initially,
    but there is no evidence that the group either under-
    stands or accepts a common objective. On the contrary,
    it is usually evident that different people have different,
    private, and personal objectives which they are attempt-
    ing to achieve in the group, and that these are often in
    conflict with each other and with the group's task.

4. People do not really listen to each other. Ideas are ig-
    nored and overridden. The discussion jumps around
    with little coherence and no sense of movement along a
    track. One gets the impression that there is much talking
    for effect—people make speeches which are obviously
    intended to impress someone else rather than being rele-
    vant to the task at hand.

    Conversation with members after the meeting will re-
    veal that they have failed to express ideas or feelings
    which they may have had for fear they would be criti-
    cized or regarded as silly. Some members feel that the
    leader or the other members are constantly making judg-
    ments of them in terms of evaluations of the contribu-
    tions they make, and so they are extremely careful about
    what they say.

5. Disagreements are generally not dealt with effectively by
    the group. They may be completely suppressed by a
    leader who fears conflict. On the other hand, they may
    result in open warfare, the consequences of which is
    domination by one subgroup over another. They may be
    "resolved" by a vote in which a very small majority wins
    the day, and a large minority remains completely
    unconvinced.

    There may be a "tyranny of the minority" in which

an individual or a small subgroup is so aggressive that the majority accedes to their wishes in order to preserve the peace or to get on with the task. In general only the more aggressive members get their ideas considered because the less aggressive people tend either to keep quiet altogether or to give up after short, ineffectual attempts to be heard.

6. Actions are often taken prematurely before the real issues are either examined or resolved. There will be much grousing after the meeting by people who disliked the decision but failed to speak up about it in the meeting itself. A simple majority is considered sufficient for action, and the minority is expected to go along. Most of the time, however, the minority remains resentful and uncommitted to the decision.

7. Action decisions tend to be unclear—no one really knows who is going to do what. Even when assignments of responsibility are made, there is often considerable doubt as to whether they will be carried out.

8. The leadership remains clearly with the committee chairman. He may be weak or strong, but he sits always "at the head of the table."

9. Criticism may be present, but it is embarrassing and tension-producing. It often appears to involve personal hostility, and the members are uncomfortable with this and unable to cope with it. Criticism of ideas tends to be destructive. Sometimes every idea proposed will be "clobbered" by someone else. Then, no one is willing to stick his neck out.

10. Personal feelings are hidden rather than being out in the open. The general attitude of the group is that these are inappropriate for discussion and would be too explosive if brought out on the table.

11. The group tends to avoid any discussion of its own "maintenance." There is often much discussion after the meeting of what was wrong and why, but these matters are seldom brought up and considered within the meeting itself where they might be resolved. [By permission

McGregor (1960) observed that there seemed to be many more
ineffective teams and wondered why this was true. He answered the
question with the following reasons: (1) We have rather low expectations of groups ("a camel is a horse designed by a committee").
(2) We do not know the ingredients of an effective team. (3) We tend
to ignore or smother the conflict which is inherent in groups. (4)
We believe the success of the team depends solely upon the leader.
(5) We do not pay attention to group maintenance or process needs.
(6) Effective teams are impossible within a Theory X management
style.

Another influential person was psychologist Rensis Likert, who
established the Institute for Social Research at the University of
Michigan. Likert studied managers and supervisors with the best
performance records to find out what worked and why. He found
that the least effective managers were "job centered" while the most
effective were "employee centered." Likert summarized his findings
into four systems of management. System 4, the most effective approach, produced high productivity and greater employee involvement. Today, we would characterize System 4 as participative or
team management. Likert's list of the twenty-four characteristics of
an effective team is similar to McGregor's formulation in that the
focus is on the process or internal dynamics of the team.

The Effective Team

1. Members are skilled in all the various leadership and
   membership roles and functions required for interaction
   between leaders and members and between members and
   other members.
2. The group has been in existence sufficiently long to have
   developed a well-established, relaxed working relationship among all its members.
3. The members of the group are attracted to it and are
   loyal to its members, including the leader.

4. The members and leaders have a high degree of confidence and trust in each other.

5. The values and goals of the group are a satisfactory integration and expression of the relevant values and needs of its members. They have helped shape these values and goals and are satisfied with them.

6. Insofar as members of the group are performing linking functions, they endeavor to have the values and goals of the groups which they link in harmony, one with the other.

7. The more important a value seems to the group, the greater the likelihood that the individual member will accept it.

8. The members of the group are highly motivated to abide by the major values and to achieve the important goals of the group. Each member will do all that he or she reasonably can—and at all times all in his or her power—to help the group achieve its central objectives. Each member expects every other member to do the same.

9. All the interaction, problem-solving, decision-making activities of the group occur in a supportive atmosphere. Suggestions, comments, ideas, information, criticisms are all offered with a helpful orientation. Similarly, these contributions are received in the same spirit. Respect is shown for the point of view of others both in the way contributions are made and in the way they are received.

10. The superior of each work group exerts a major influence in establishing the tone and atmosphere of that work group by his or her leadership principles and practices. In the highly effective group, consequently, the leader adheres to those principles of leadership which create a supportive atmosphere in the group and a cooperative rather than a competitive relationship among the members.

11. The group is eager to help each member develop to his or her full potential. It sees, for example, that relevant

technical knowledge and training in interpersonal and
group skills are made available to each member.

12. Each member accepts willingly and without resentment
the goals and expectations that the individual and the
group establish for themselves. The anxieties, fears, and
emotional stresses produced by direct pressure for high
performance from a boss in a hierarchical situation are
not present. Groups seem capable of setting high performance goals for the group as a whole and for each
member. These goals are high enough to stimulate each
member to do his or her best, but not so high as to create
anxieties or fear of failure. In an effective group, each
person can exert sufficient influence on the decisions of
the group to prevent the group from setting unattainable
goals for any member while setting high goals for all.
The goals are adapted to the member's capacity to
perform.

13. The leader and the members believe that each group
member can accomplish the "impossible." These expectations stretch each member to the maximum and accel-
erate personal growth. When necessary, the group
tempers the expectation level so that the member is not
broken by a feeling of failure or rejection.

14. When necessary or advisable, other members of the
group will give a member the help needed to accomplish
successfully the goals set for that person. Mutual help is
a characteristic of highly effective groups.

15. The supportive atmosphere of the highly effective group
stimulates creativity. The group does not demand narrow conformity as do the work groups under authori-
tarian leaders. No one has to "yes the boss," nor is a
person rewarded for such an attempt. The group at-
taches high value to new, creative approaches and solutions to its problems and to the problems of the
organization of which it is a part.

16. The group knows the value of "constructive" conformity and knows when to use it and for what purposes.
Although it does not permit conformity to affect adverse-

ly the creative efforts of its members, it does expect conformity on mechanical and administrative matters to save the time of members and to facilitate the group's activities.

17.   There is strong motivation on the part of each member to communicate fully and frankly to the group all the information which is relevant and of value to the group's activity.

18.   There is high motivation in the group to use the communication process so that it best serves the interests and goals of the group. Every item which a member feels is important, but which for some reason is being ignored, will be repeated until it receives the attention that it deserves. Members strive also to avoid communicating unimportant information so as not to waste the group's time.

19.   Just as there is high motivation to communicate, there is correspondingly strong motivation to receive communications. Each member is genuinely interested in any information on any relevant matter that any member of the group can provide. This information is welcomed and trusted as being honestly and sincerely given. Members do not look "behind" information and attempt to interpret it in ways opposite to its purported intent.

20.   In the highly effective group, there are strong motivations to try to influence other members as well as to be receptive to influence by them. This applies to all the group's activities: technical matters, methods, organizational problems, interpersonal relationships, and group processes.

21.   The group processes of the highly effective group enable the members to exert more influence on the leader and to communicate far more information to him or her, including suggestions as to what needs to be done and how the leader could do a better job, than is possible in a one-to-one relationship. By "tossing the ball" back and forth among the members, a group can communicate

information to the leader which no single person on a
one-to-one basis dare do.

22.   The ability of the members of a group to influence each
      other contributes to the flexibility and adaptability of the
      group. Ideas, goals and attitudes do not become frozen if
      members are able to influence each other continuously.

23.   In the highly effective group, individual members feel
      secure in making decisions which seem appropriate to
      them because the goals and philosophy of operation are
      clearly understood by each member and provide a solid
      base for making decisions. This unleashes initiative and
      pushes decisions down while still maintaining a coordi-
      nated and directed effort.

24.   The leader of a highly effective group is selected care-
      fully. His or her leadership ability is so evident that he
      or she would probably emerge as a leader in any unstruc-
      tured situation. To increase the likelihood that persons
      of high leadership competence are selected, the organi-
      zation is likely to use peer nominations and related
      methods in selecting group leaders. [By permission from
      New Patterns of Management, by R. Likert. Copyright
      1961. McGraw-Hill.]

The psychologist Chris Argyris focused his attention on the personal development of the individual in the context of the organization. Organizational effectiveness, Argyris (1964, pp. 139–140)
believed, was a function of the interpersonal competence of team
members and the extent to which the organization supported positive norms. Positive team norms are the following:

1.   To be candid about ideas and feelings
2.   To be open
3.   To experiment
4.   To help others to be candid about their ideas and feelings
5.   To help others to be open
6.   To help others to experiment
7.   Individuality
8.   Thought

9. Concern
10. Internal commitment

Argyris pointed to the team-member behaviors required for effective teamwork. While his focus was also on internal process, his emphasis on candor, experimentation, and individuality was helpful in giving emphasis to the need for team players who are willing to challenge the status quo.

The work of Robert Blake and Jane Mouton is extremely important because it links management style and team effectiveness in a concept called the Managerial Grid (Blake and Mouton, 1964).

The Grid clarifies and crystallizes many of the fundamentals of behavior dynamics in business. Here is the basis of it. Any man who is working for a firm has assigned responsibilities. This is true whether he works at a very low level or high up in the organization. Whenever he acts as a manager, there are two matters on his mind. One is production—the results of his efforts. How much he thinks about results can be described as his degree of concern for production. The horizontal axis of the Grid stands for concern for production. It is a nine-point continuum, where 9 shows high concern for production and 1, low concern. A manager is also thinking about those around him, either bosses, colleagues, or those whose work he directs. The vertical axis represents his concern for people. This, too, is on a nine-point continuum with 9, a high degree and 1, a low degree.

The Grid reflects these two concerns. It does so in a way that enables men to comprehend how the two concerns interact. At points of intersection are theories. They are theories that every manager uses when he thinks about how to get results through people, whether he realizes it or not [Blake and Mouton, 1969, p. 60].

In the upper-right-hand corner of the Grid is the 9.9 manager. This style is characterized by a high concern for both people (process) and production (task). A person with this style emphasizes fact-finding and an open discussion of issues as the keys to effective problem solving and decision making. A team of 9.9 people will work interdependently and will seek full commitment to their decision before proceeding.

The Grid is used to improve overall team effectiveness as well as the individual effectiveness of each team member. Grid team building involves an analysis of the current team criteria in terms of planning, problem solving, communication, and other dimensions of an effective team in the context of the Grid. Team building also includes feedback from team members on their perceptions of each person's Grid style in actual team situations. Structured experiences help team members apply this information, and the net result of this phase of Grid development is a plan for team and individual improvement. Blake and Mouton gave us a model of team excellence and a set of styles useful in understanding team-member contributions.

Other contributions have been helpful in understanding teamwork and team players. Richard Walton (1969) provided a helpful distinction between types of conflict that may arise among team members. Substantive conflict involves disagreements about roles, procedures, and policies and can be dealt with by discussion and negotiation. Emotional conflict arises from feelings of loss, fear, and mistrust. While there is often overlap, it is helpful to identify the underlying causes of internal team conflicts. Role analysis techniques and role negotiations are two techniques designed to deal with conflicts of this type (Dayal and Thomas, 1968; Harrison, 1971). William Dyer's (1987) *Team Building: Issues and Alternatives* offers a variety of techniques for managers and consultants who facilitate team-building events.

More recently the focus has been on leadership. Considerable attention has been given to defining leadership and to distinguishing between management and leadership. From the standpoint of team effectiveness, the most important contribution has been the emphasis on the future through an inspired view often called *visioning*. Organizations (and teams) require a person who will create or help the team develop a picture of where they want to be in years ahead (Bennis and Nanus, 1985; Block, 1987; Kouzes and Posner, 1987). In an era that emphasizes quality results, cost-cutting efficiencies, and other short-term solutions, teams need to maintain a broad, long-term, conceptual view.

Much of this discussion of teamwork, and most of the early research, was based upon studies conducted in the private sector. However, all of the concepts are also applicable to the public and nonprofit sectors. More recently, attention has been given to the organization development in the public and nonprofit world (Golembiewski and Eddy, 1978; Schmuck, Runkel, and Langmeier, 1969; Beckard, 1974).

As we acknowledge the more important contributions by behavioral scientists and others, it is necessary to note that the organizational environment changed dramatically during the 1980s. There are new operating rules. Therefore, as we approach the twenty-first century, we need a comprehensive model of effective teamwork:

- Positive norms emerging from the informal system must be complemented by the policies and procedures of the formal organization.
- Process behaviors that build and maintain the team must work hand in hand with activities that promote the completion of basic team tasks.
- An informal, relaxed internal team climate must be coupled with a parallel concern for building effective relationships with key players outside the team.
- A concern for production and people must be seen in the context of a shared vision and long-term goals.
- A team vision, mission statement, and goals are of limited value unless backed up by a road map of action steps.
- Mission, goals, and action plans can become derailed by a failure to clarify role expectations of team members.

A New Model of Effectiveness

Twelve characteristics or behaviors distinguish effective teams from ineffective teams. You get a certain feeling when you are part of a solid team. You enjoy being around the people, you look forward to all meetings, you learn new things, you laugh more, you find yourself putting the team's assignments ahead of other work, and you feel a real sense of progress and accomplishment. In the final analysis, effective teams are composed of effective team players. The twelve characteristics of an effective team come alive when team members are high-performing team players. In this chapter, we outline the characteristics of an effective team and the role of team players. Table 2 presents a summary of the characteristics. In the next chapter we present four team-player styles and discuss how each contributes to effective teamwork.

Clear Sense of Purpose. Call it a mission, goal, charter, or task, but a team must know why it exists and what it should be doing at the end of a day's meeting, by the end of the quarter, at year's end, or perhaps five years from now. There are few more frustrating activities than being part of a group (masquerading as a team) that meets with no sense of why they have come together. In some organizations, employees are part of a unit because of what I call "administrative convenience." Everyone has to be somewhere in the company's hierarchy, but sometimes the rationale for the placement is not clear.

In a recent team-building session, a division management team spent three days formulating their mission—a statement outlining their basic products and services and their principal customers. While the meetings that led to the mission statement were difficult and tiring, operating without a shared understanding of the team's purpose was significantly more frustrating. No one likes to be part of something that is not going anywhere.

In my experience, teams that have existed for years often operate as if there were a common agreement on purpose. When the question "Why do we exist?" is raised and discussed, usually the quick answer is "To share information." However, there is often a lack of unity on such issues as overall purpose and role expectations and on procedural questions such as decision making, communication methods, and interfaces with other teams.

Teams often find it useful to create a shared vision. The visioning process, mentioned earlier, involves defining your preferred future. This is significantly different from your prediction of the future—what you think it will be.

In my workshops on goal setting and in my consulting assign-

Table 2. Characteristics of an Effective Team.

1. Clear Purpose	The vision, mission, goal, or task of the team has been defined and is now accepted by everyone. There is an action plan.
2. Informality	The climate tends to be informal, comfortable, and relaxed. There are no obvious tensions or signs of boredom.
3. Participation	There is much discussion and everyone is encouraged to participate.
4. Listening	The members use effective listening techniques such as questioning, paraphrasing, and summarizing to get out ideas.
5. Civilized Disagreement	There is disagreement, but the team is comfortable with this and shows no signs of avoiding, smoothing over, or suppressing conflict.
6. Consensus Decisions	For important decisions, the goal is substantial but not necessarily unanimous agreement through open discussion of everyone's ideas, avoidance of formal voting, or easy compromises.
7. Open Communication	Team members feel free to express their feelings on the tasks as well as on the group's operation. There are few hidden agendas. Communication takes place outside of meetings.
8. Clear Roles and Work Assignments	There are clear expectations about the roles played by each team member. When action is taken, clear assignments are made, accepted, and carried out. Work is fairly distributed among team members.
9. Shared Leadership	While the team has a formal leader, leadership functions shift from time to time depending upon the circumstances, the needs of the group, and the skills of the members. The formal leader models the appropriate behavior and helps establish positive norms.
10. External Relations	The team spends time developing key outside relationships, mobilizing resources, and building credibility with important players in other parts of the organization.
11. Style Diversity	The team has a broad spectrum of team-player types including members who emphasize attention to task, goal setting, focus on process, and questions about how the team is functioning.
12. Self-Assessment	Periodically, the team stops to examine how well it is functioning and what may be interfering with its effectiveness.

ments with management teams, I help people create visions with a series of exercises. Creating a vision is somewhat like brainstorming—a no-holds-barred, free-form, creative thinking process. In one exercise, I ask team members to close their eyes to imagine it is five years from now and they are in a helicopter hovering over their organization. Then I ask them to look down and get a picture of what they would like to see—not what they expect to see. Each person writes down or draws a picture of the elements of his or her vision. The team then prepares a shared vision drawn from outputs of the exercise. The vision becomes the focus of all succeeding efforts—mission statement, goals, objectives, and action plans.

Effective teams are clear about their daily tasks and about agenda items for meetings. Although it is important to create a shared vision and mission, the success of most teams is dependent upon their ability to focus on the task at hand. Therefore, every meeting must have a detailed agenda, and members should be prepared with the information necessary to discuss all agenda items. Team members should help to control the time of the meeting, and only emergency interruptions should be allowed. And, of course, minutes should be kept to record decisions and assignments.

Team players play an important role in creating a clear sense of purpose by

- Insisting that the team have a vision of the future, develop a mission, prepare goals and objectives, and then periodically revisit them
- Creating milestone charts and task assignments
- Ensuring the involvement of all members in development of the team's purpose
- Pushing the team to reach for "stretch" goals and objectives

Informal Climate. The atmosphere tends to be informal, comfortable, and relaxed. There are no obvious signs of boredom or tension.

One signal that your team is effective is that you enjoy being around the people. You want to come to the team meetings. You look forward to all associations and contacts with other team members. You know the feeling because you have had the opposite feeling so many times. When you are part of a poorly functioning team, your reaction to receiving the meeting notice is usually something like "ugh." You dread the team get-togethers and find yourself looking for excuses to avoid the meetings and other contacts with team members.

A team with a positive climate bypasses the formal trappings such as rigid voting rules and raising hands before speaking. Rather, an obvious ease of interaction and communication relaxes team members and enhances their contributions. Members feel comfortable speaking with each other regardless of position, age, sex, or race.

Humor seems to be an integral part of successful teams. Members talk about team meetings as "enjoyable," and "fun," and even "a lot of laughs." When the environment is relaxed and informal, people feel free to engage in good-natured kidding, social banter about events unrelated to work, and anecdotes regarding recent company business.

Look around at some of your best teams and assess the degree of formality. You will notice that team members often come early to the meetings because they enjoy the informal chatting over coffee prior to the meeting. And the pleasant looks on members' faces are indicators that they enjoy being there. After the meeting, they will usually stay for a while to continue the discussion or just to trade stories. I have noticed that effective teams schedule meetings at times that facilitate the informal aspects. For example:

- First thing in the morning, beginning with time for coffee and socializing
- Just prior to noon, followed by a lunch together
- At the end of the day, backed up by a cocktail party or an informal get-together at a nearby restaurant

Team players help create an informal climate by:

- Offering to provide the team with the necessary resources without waiting for a formal request
- Being willing to share the limelight with other members when the team is successful

- Helping members to get to know and feel comfortable with each other
- Using humor and discussions of subjects other than work to relieve tension and smooth over awkward moments

Participation. Team membership based upon the demands of the group's task will result in extensive member involvement in the group's discussions and activities. In short, everyone participates.

Although effective teams will have all team members actively participating, participation will vary; that is, not everyone will participate equally or in the same manner. I have observed and charted the participation levels of many teams. As a result, I am a firm believer in the concept of *weighted participation.* This concept holds that it is the quality and, more important, the impact of the participation that must be calculated. While clearly this is a subjective measurement (as opposed to the simple counting of the number of times a team member speaks), a trained observer can easily make a judgment about contributions.

I have observed one business team for many years, and one member comes to mind who reflects weighted participation in its purest sense. Jack is economical in his communication. He speaks only four or five times in a two-hour meeting. He wastes few words, gets to the point, and does not repeat himself. Jack's participation usually has impact because he provides useful information the team needs at the time, summarizes the key points, conclusions, or tentative decisions, or simply points out how the group has been wasting time and needs to move on.

Other team members participate extensively but not always in the verbal discussions. You can tell they are involved because they participate nonverbally by nodding, leaning forward, and taking notes. Some team members will prepare reports, handouts, and presentations while others will set up the meeting room, get the necessary equipment, or arrange for an outside speaker or tape.

The type of participation may vary, and it is important to measure both the manner and impact to determine if your team meets the test of extensive participation. The objective of effective participation is to encourage all team members to participate. Another key participation indicator, therefore, is opportunity. Effective teams provide all members with an opportunity to participate. Conversely, we have all known teams in which a few people dominated the action and limited the participation of other team members.

Participation can be enhanced by team players who:

- Limit their participation to the agenda item under consideration
- Intervene when the participation is not relevant to the task
- Encourage silent members to participate in the discussion
- Speak out even when their views are contrary to the majority

Participation should be relevant to the goal or task of the team. Teams often engage in a great deal of talk, but much of it is off the mark. I have worked with a number of teams in which there was a great deal of good-natured kidding, story telling, and discussions of personal life. The members genuinely enjoyed each other and looked forward to the interaction that accompanied team meetings. Unfortunately, very little work was accomplished, few decisions were reached, and progress toward organizational goals was minimal. And my interventions, which were directed toward making the discussions more task relevant, were met with strong objections. They resented my implication that they are not an effective team. "We're communicating, aren't we?" was a typical team-member response. Beneath the surface was the belief that any changes in the team would destroy the delicate balance that was keeping the group from coming apart. Often, there were deep divisions that were being covered by the humor and trivial discussions.

Dealing with nonrelevant participation can be tricky. We want an informal, relaxed climate, but it must be combined with a focus on goals and tasks at hand. My approach has been to get the team to address their degree of satisfaction with accomplishments or progress toward goals. Interviews, surveys, or guided group discussions are simple but effective techniques for collecting data about participation and its relationship to team effectiveness.

Listening. The single most important factor distinguishing effective from ineffective teams is the ability of team members to listen to each other. It is a skill that serves as an underpinning for all the other determinants of effectiveness. Sadly, this is one area that gets more lip service than action. While everyone agrees that listening skills are important, little is done to develop that capacity in team members.

I am intrigued by the popularity of workshops in memory development, business writing, speed reading, and public speaking, and by the corresponding lack of interest in listening-skills seminars. The assumption is, I suspect, that if your auditory system is functioning, you are able to listen effectively.

There are four communication skills: (1) reading, (2) writing, (3) speaking, and (4) listening. This list presents the four skills in a rank order based upon the amount of time the average person spends in training to develop the skill. Unfortunately, this list is an inverse ranking of the degree to which adults need to use the skills in the business world. In other words, listening and speaking are more widely used and more valuable capabilities than are writing and reading. Therefore, we have the problem and unfortunate situation of the communication skills in greatest demand receiving the least resources for training and development.

The principal listening skill is the ability to sit back, be attentive, and take in what is said while reserving judgment. We can absorb and process words spoken by other people much faster than they can verbalize the information. This leaves us lots of time to analyze, evaluate, and even anticipate their thoughts. But this extra time can be a disadvantage since we tend to concentrate minimally on what is being said and often discount comments before they are completed. The ability to listen and reserve judgment is critical if all ideas are to be given adequate consideration. This skill is especially important for team problem solving and decision making.

Another important listening skill is the capacity for active listening. Active listening takes a variety of forms. In its most basic and perhaps most powerful manifestation, team members react nonverbally to the contributions of others by nodding, maintaining eye contact, and leaning forward. They may add short verbal acknowledgments such as "I see" and "uh huh." Active listening is all the more powerful because it so rarely happens. Therefore, when someone really listens, you are doubly impressed—with yourself and with the other person. The person is saying "I'm interested in what you have to say."

An ancillary active listening skill is paraphrasing expressed facts and feelings. Sometimes called *reflecting,* the classic response begins, "What I hear you saying is . . ." Or "You seem upset about . . ." The goal of paraphrasing or reflecting is (1) to make sure you are clear about what is intended by the other team member and (2) to let the other person know you care about what he or she is communicating.

We have all had the experience of using words that we knew were not really communicating to other team members what we were feeling or thinking. The techniques of active listening are strong tools for helping all team members find the right words to express their thoughts or feelings and to maximize their contributions to the team effort.

In another sense, active listening helps team players develop self-understanding. In the process of explaining their thoughts, the team members often come to a better understanding of the issue. In short, we are providing them with a chance to alter their thoughts and feelings. Table 3 provides some examples of the uses of active listening.

Team players can support the norm of high-level listening by:

- Reserving judgment on a presentation until all the data are presented and analyzed
- Being willing to learn and act on opinions and facts that may alter the team mission or goals
- Modeling the effective listening skills (for example, paraphrasing) for other team members
- Summarizing and acknowledging when their views differ from those of other team members

Civilized Disagreement. Disagreement is, of course, a euphemism for conflict. We tend to shy away from the word *conflict* because it connotes negative behavior or, at the very least, an unpleasant relationship. We have developed many of our feelings about the word because of media headlines such as "Middle-East conflict," "labor-management conflict," and "conflict between city hall and the gay community." Therefore, conflict is portrayed as war and, as a result, a situation to be avoided. In terms of effective teamwork, nothing

Table 3. Active Listening.

Use of Active Listening	Examples
1. To convey interest in what the other person is saying	I see!
2. To encourage the individual to expand further on his or her thinking	Yes, go on. Tell us more.
3. To help the individual clarify the problem in his or her own thinking	Then the problem as you see it is . . .
4. To get the individual to hear what he or she has said in the way it sounded to others	This is your decision then, and the reasons are . . . If I understand you correctly, you are saying that we should . . .
5. To pull out the key ideas from a long statement or discussion	Your major point is . . . You feel that we should . . .
6. To respond to a person's feelings more than to his or her words	You feel strongly that . . . You do not believe that . . .
7. To summarize specific points of agreement and disagreement as a basis for further discussion	We seem to be agreed on the following points . . . , but we seem to need further clarification on these points . . .
8. To express a consensus of group feeling	As a result of this discussion, we as a group seem to feel that . . .

could be further from the truth. Conflicts will occur. The problem is that these conflicts usually are not resolved satisfactorily; most groups have not learned the requisite conflict-resolution skills.

Disagreements are to be encouraged and accepted as a natural consequence of a dynamic, active organization. Effective teams create a climate in which people feel free to express their opinions even when those opinions are at odds with those of other team members.

Problems often arise from the manner in which an opinion is expressed. Attacking another team member, denigrating the opposite position, a hostile tone or voice, or an aggressive hand gesture can lead to destructive conflict. In short, we get uncivilized disagree-

Table 4. Aspects of Conflict.

Destructive	*Constructive*
Diverts energy from more important activities and issues	Opens up issues of importance resulting in their clarification
Destroys the morale of people or reinforces poor self-concepts	Results in the solution of problems
Polarizes groups so they increase internal cohesiveness and reduce intergroup cooperation	Increases the involvement of individuals in issues of importance to them
Deepens differences in values	Causes authentic communication to occur
Produces irresponsible and regrettable behavior such as name-calling and fighting	Serves as a release for pent-up emotion, anxiety, and stress
	Helps build cohesiveness among people sharing the conflict, celebrating in its settlement, and learning more about each other
	Helps individuals grow personally and apply what they learn to future situations

Source: Adapted from Hart, 1980, p. 6.

ment. Clearly, as indicated in Table 4, conflict can be destructive or constructive.

Effective teams want differences to be expressed, and members use their communication and listening skills to ensure that all points surface. They see diversity as a strength of the team. As a result, team members are supported in their efforts to articulate their ideas, to come forth with contrary information, and to discuss their feelings in a positive manner.

Conflict, therefore, has become a dirty word because differences often linger unresolved, leading the parties to become contentious, or because the outcome is arrived at in such a manner that no one feels satisfied.

I have encountered five different methods of resolving conflicts: denial, smoothing over, power, compromise, and problem solving.

When *denial* is operating, team members simply do not recognize or, more accurately, do not acknowledge the existence of any dissension. They simply go about their business, often going on to the next agenda item without the blink of an eye. If someone on the team asks about the "problem," other team members will refer to the matter as a "healthy discussion" or "good exchange of ideas" and then move on.

Smoothing over is the first cousin of denial, although here the conflict or difference of opinion is admitted but characterized as "trivial." Team members are advised not to worry about it, but, of course, everybody secretly wishes that it would go away. There is a strong feeling among some people that talking about problems, feelings, and conflicts only makes them worse. A favorite ploy to smother conflict is the use of humor. Tension among colleagues may make other team members uncomfortable, and joking relieves the tension. But it can lead to avoidance of any serious consideration of the issues. Humor is important to the success of a team, but in excess, it can detract from the group's mission, and when misused, it can deter discussion of important problems.

The third method of resolving conflicts is use of *power*. The simplest, cleanest, and easiest way is for one person to decide the outcome. One team member may be the boss or in some other way may have control over the behavior of the others. Therefore, when conflicts arise, members of the team turn to this person for "the word." In a more subtle version of the power game, team members discuss their differences, and it may appear that some real team problem solving is taking place. Then, when a deadline approaches or the meeting is about to end, the "power" steps in with a decision to "save time" or "move along."

Compromise is the most deceptive and seductive method of conflict resolution. Like cotton candy, it looks good on the outside, but when you are finished, it is not very satisfying. Compromise, in its crudest form, is "splitting the differences." In other words, you believe the team should meet six times a year while I think four meetings are sufficient. After some discussion, we settle on five meetings, and on the surface, this decision looks great. However, neither of us is satisfied; we have just minimized our dissatisfaction. More important, we have not worked toward a decision that is best for our team; rather, we have worked toward a decision that is acceptable. Compromise is used when team members want to reduce the extent of the conflict and avoid the work associated with problem solving.

Problem solving, sometimes called collaborative conflict resolution, is the most difficult but potentially the most satisfying method. This approach requires that team members acknowledge that some differences exist, agree to deal with the issues and not smooth them over, forgo power as a quick and easy alternative, and avoid simple compromises when the problems are complex and important.

Effective problem solving begins with a discussion leading ultimately to an agreement on a problem statement. This discussion may involve an examination of where we are now versus where we want to be. In other contexts, we talk about degree of nonconformance, plan versus actual, or current condition against standard. Sometimes the development of a problem statement involves constructing the ideal or desired state, as in "How would it look if there were no communications problems?"

The next step is problem analysis. This is when we want the participation of team members who have data and opinions. Research and study by team members may also be necessary.

Generating alternative solutions is an important step that is often overlooked. Too often, teams jump to the first available answer without considering other possibilities. Few problems have only one possible solution. Solution selection should involve as many team members as possible. While the team needs a diversity of ideas, the team's commitment to the ultimate solution is equally important. Participation in the decision process will help ensure the team's support for the implementation of the solution.

This collaborative approach to conflict resolution moves a team toward a search for the best response to a problem. Successful application of this method also leads to strengthening the team and increases group cohesion. Team players can establish a climate for civilized disagreement by:

- Maintaining an objective, analytical approach to the differences
- Being flexible and open to all points of view
- Diffusing overt hostility through the use of humor

- Backing off when their views are not being accepted by the rest
  of the team

Consensus. A centerpiece of the effective team is the use of the
consensus method for making key decisions. A consensus requires
unity but not unanimity and concurrence but not consistency. The
problem-solving approach to conflict resolution implies differences
among team members, and consensus is the technique to reach
agreement about the problem statement and the recommended solution. Here is how it works:

> In a steering committee meeting, the group had to decide on
> the format for an upcoming company conference. Bruce
> argued strongly for an overnight session because it would al-
> low sufficient social time after the meetings to facilitate infor-
> mal get-togethers, which he felt were important for improving
> intergroup communication. The other committee members
> agreed with the need for the social aspect but felt the lodging
> costs would not be viewed positively by upper management.
> As an alternative, they proposed a one-day conference ending
> at 4:00 P.M. followed by a two-hour cocktail party. Bruce still
> felt the overnight was preferable but went along with the one-
> day alternative as "the best approach, given the current cost
> containment environment." A consensus had been reached.

A consensus is reached when all members can say they either
agree with the decision or have had their "day in court" and were
unable to convince the others of their viewpoint. In the final analysis, everyone agrees to support the outcome. It is not a majority
because that implies a vote, and voting is verboten for teams using
the consensus method. Voting tends to split the group into winners
and losers, thereby creating needless divisions. Consensus does not
require unanimity since members may still disagree with the final
result but are willing to work toward its success. This is the hallmark of a team player. Table 5 provides some tips for successful use
of the consensus method.

Horse-trading is a variation of the compromise approach to conflict resolution. It means that I got something that was important

Table 5. Using the Consensus Method.

Do's	Don't's
Use active listening skills	Horse-trade
Involve as many members as possible	Vote
Seek out the reasons behind arguments; dig for the facts	Agree just to avoid "rocking the boat"

to me on the last round, so this time I will go along with your pet project. To get the best decisions, teams must avoid even subtle horse-trading.

One of the major arguments against the consensus method is that it is too time-consuming. It is true that it takes longer than the autocratic (one person decides) and democratic (majority vote) systems. However, autocratic and democratic decisions often unravel because the team does not truly support the outcome, so members are unwilling to put forth the effort required for successful implementation.

I remember a workshop participant once telling me, "Glenn, this consensus approach is fine. But I just do not want a pilot on my next flight having a nice group discussion with the crew when the plane is having engine problems and in danger of crashing. I want one person in charge."

This sounds right, but research and practice in the airline industry clearly indicate the need for more teamwork in the cockpit. There are few situations in which a split-second decision is required. In most cases, time is available to collect data, share ideas, and make a decision. The statistics on the causes of fatal accidents and near misses are so powerful that several airlines have taken action to develop cockpit management skills and to improve teamwork among airline personnel. The now infamous Eastern Airline flight 401, which crashed near Miami in 1972 killing some 150 people, is used as a case study of poor team management. Pilots are taught participative management skills and other crew members learn how to be more assertive.

The consensus approach has its place even in difficult situations, but it is not always appropriate. It must be used judiciously. Your team should use the consensus technique when:

- There is no clear answer.
- There is no single expert in the group.
- Commitment to the decision is essential.
- Sufficient time is available.

Consensus decisions can be facilitated by team players who:

- Press for reasons and data to support decisions
- Discourage the use of other decision-making tactics (for example, voting and one-person rule)
- Periodically summarize and test possible decisions with the group
- Are willing to go along with the team's consensus even though they may disagree with it

Open Communication. A company president complained to me that all his management board meetings were too cheerful. "Everyone is so polite to each other," he remarked. Conflicts existed among the vice-presidents but were never addressed. There was a low level of trust among the group resulting in a reluctance to discuss openly key issues. Individual vice-presidents talked to the president about their problems with other VPs and hoped the president would handle them (meaning that he would talk to the other person).

Trust is clearly the avenue to open communication. Members must have confidence that they can reveal aspects of themselves and their work without fear of reprisals or embarrassment. The higher the level of trust, the more risks team members are willing to take.

When a new team forms, typically the level of trust among all members is low. They are defensive and interact with each other from their formal role positions. They are testing each other, norms of acceptable behavior are forming, and safety in interpersonal relations is the goal. The formal leader tends to be more controlling as he or she exercises considerable leadership authority.

Initially, the flow of communication is distorted as team

members "play their cards close to the vest." As the team matures, trust increases with a corresponding increase in openness, in confrontation of issues, and in the use of influence skills. At the outset, goal setting and planning are often competitive activities as team members are intent on winning a game of wits. Later, as they are able to level with each other, the team adopts a problem-solving mode in which members are open to learning from each other. (Chapter Six includes a comprehensive discussion of the stages of team development.)

Team players can encourage open communication and trust by:

- Being dependable—someone on whom the team can rely to deliver on commitments
- Pitching in and helping other team members who need assistance
- Reading and responding to nonverbal cues that suggest a lack of openness
- Candidly sharing views and encouraging others to do the same

The leader's behavior is crucial in building trust and opening communication. First, the leader must encourage discussion of problems and key issues and then model a response that is nonjudgmental. It must be seen as OK to ask for help or to seek the advice of other team members. Second, the leader should support (and feel comfortable with) the concept of subgroups of team members working together. This decontrolling is critical for group growth. The goal is shared leadership whereby all members take responsibility for ensuring the success of the team by performing leadership functions on an as-needed basis. This process relieves the formal leader of the burden of doing it all and empowers the team.

Clear Roles and Work Assignments. Every team member has a formal job with a series of functions often defined in a job description or specification. The concept of *role* goes beyond a listing of tasks to the expectations a specific team member has about his or her job and to the expectations that other team members have about that job. Since effective teamwork involves task interdependence, agreement on these expectations is extremely important. The work of the team will not be optimized if team members do not know what others expect of them or if there is a conflict in expectations.

During interviews in preparation for team building with a group of health professionals, it became clear to me that role conflict was the problem. I asked all team members how they viewed the critical jobs on the team. In summarizing the interview data, it became clear that there were widely varying expectations of several of the key players. A number of techniques for clarifying expectations were available, but I elected to use a brief version of role negotiations (Harrison, 1971) in which each team member enlists the aid of other members in doing his or her job more effectively. These requests brought out some expectations that had not been communicated previously and some other expectations that were conflicting or difficult to implement. A process of clarification, exploring alternatives, and agreement culminated in a series of "contracts" among team members. In the final analysis, conflicts that were surfacing as personality differences turned out to be conflicts in role expectations.

Awareness of the importance of roles is essential to the success of a team. Teams often see conflicts among their members on the emotional (feelings) level when, in fact, the conflict is substantive (roles, procedures). Role conflict and ambiguity can cause considerable stress on the team and can result in lost productivity, dissatisfaction, and a tendency of members to leave the team.

Role clarification is important at any time. It is useful when (1) as in this case, data collection reveals a diagnosis of role conflict or ambiguity, (2) a new team is forming, or (3) a new member joins the team.

A great deal of teamwork takes place outside of team meetings. In order for teams to be effective, they must make clear-cut decisions and plan necessary follow-up actions.

In my experience, the most successful teams are those in which team members take responsibility for work assignments critical to the achievement of the team's mission. They volunteer for jobs such as data collection, drafting reports, preparing presentations, and setting up meetings.

Assignments must also be completed on time. Effective team players are committed to the team, and as a result, they would not dare come unprepared to a meeting. In fact, one of the best teams I have experienced has a norm that strongly encourages team members to send all reports, background materials, and other relevant information out to the team in advance of the next meeting. This procedure helps the team save time during the meetings and allows members to be prepared for team decisions.

One key test for team effectiveness is the extent to which task assignments are distributed among team members. The negative effects of a team in which a few people carry the load quickly become obvious. At first, things seem very efficient, and a great deal of work gets done. Soon, however, these people experience burnout or, worse, resentment toward other team members. Eventually, this kind of team deteriorates into a loose group with a small core of workers and others who are members in name only.

Members of effective teams never say, "That's not my job." When team members realize that one of their colleagues has an especially difficult or time-consuming assignment, they offer to pitch in and help. One situation that illustrated this point was an assignment to locate an appropriate conference facility for an off-site company meeting. This assignment was difficult because of certain location, facilities, and budget constraints. One team member volunteered to conduct the basic research of contacting a number of potential conference centers and collecting information. She then turned over the information to the responsible team member who used the data for analysis and subsequent negotiations.

Another team I know of does not allow team members to send substitutes to the meetings. This rule tends to ensure that all assignments are completed on time because team members cannot skip a meeting if they have not done their homework.

Effective role clarification and assignments occur when team players:

- Push the team to set high quality standards for work contributed by members
- Are willing to work outside their defined roles when necessary
- Ensure that assignments are evenly distributed among team members

- Openly discuss and negotiate their expectations of each team member's role

Shared Leadership. All teams have a formal leader. A variety of titles are used to designate the position: manager, supervisor, coach, chairperson, coordinator, captain, director, or, simply, the boss. Traditionally, we give a great deal of authority and, accordingly, much responsibility to the leader for the success of the team. This is just plain wrong. Over the long haul, a team will not be successful if the leader carries the sole responsibility for ensuring that the team reaches its goals. Leadership of a team must be shared among team members. Everyone must feel and take responsibility for meeting the task and process needs of the team. If the team fails, everybody fails. This is one of the most important concepts of team effectiveness, but it is also the most difficult to teach.

Clearly, it is easier and, for many people, more desirable to have someone who will tell us what to do, when to do it, and how to do it. And it is convenient to have someone to blame! One of the most frustrating things for me is to leave a team meeting and meet a member in the hall who says, "Well, wasn't that a waste of time?" My response is always the same: "Don't bring it up to me after the meeting. This does no good at all. Next time, say something during the meeting when it counts. It is your team, your meeting, your valuable time, and, therefore, your responsibility to do whatever it takes (for example, ask the group to stick to the agenda) to help ensure it is not a waste of time."

In many situations, the formal leader is either unaware of or unable to exercise the required leadership function at the time it is needed. And I did use the word *leadership* to describe the activity. In its most basic form, leadership is any action that helps a team reach its goals. Members of successful teams use words such as *our* and *we* when referring to their teams.

In successful teams, leadership is shared. While the formal leader has certain administrative, legal, and bureaucratic responsibilities, leadership functions shift from time to time among team members, depending upon the needs of the group and the skills of the members. Behavioral scientists have categorized these functions as task responsibilities and process responsibilities.

As the name implies, *task responsibilities* are actions that help the team reach its goal, accomplish an immediate task, make a decision, or solve a problem. Teams tend to be most effective in this area because, by training and temperament, people are more task oriented. Most role models and most training in education and business settings focus on what to do to accomplish a task. Consider all the books and workshops on such topics as time management, meeting planning, and goal setting.

For *process responsibilities,* the emphasis is on how we go about accomplishing our task. It is the interpersonal glue that helps maintain or, better yet, exploit all our team's resources. On the whole, teams tend to be less process oriented because traditional training stresses such axioms as "The end justifies the means" and "Winning is everything." Effective teams, however, know that the quality of their decisions is impacted by the manner in which they make their judgments.

Team players can help establish the norm of shared leadership by ensuring that both the task and process functions are addressed by the team. Some examples are found in Table 6.

External Relations. In *The Superteam Solution,* Hastings, Bixby, and Chaudhry-Lawton (1987) made us aware of the "importance of the invisible team"—customers, clients, users, and sponsors. These other players make demands on the team, provide access to needed resources, and are a source of valuable feedback on team performance.

The resources of customers and clients are important indicators of success. Tom Peters has provided many examples of companies that regularly ask customers, "How are we doing?" (Peters, 1987). In the data processing field, there are many user groups and joint developer-user committees.

Teams usually need a sponsor who can serve as godfather, mentor, and promoter. A good sponsor can increase the life of a team and provide access to needed resources (budget, staff, publicity).

Multidisciplinary teams need the cooperation of the functional departments from which team members are drawn. The managers of the functional departments can support the team by encouraging their people to give all assignments a high priority. In addition,

Table 6. Leadership Responsibilities.

Task	Process
1. Initiating: proposing tasks, goals, or actions; defining group problems; suggesting a procedure	1. Harmonizing: attempting to reconcile disagreements; reducing tension; getting people to explore differences
2. Offering Facts: giving expression of feeling; giving an opinion	2. Gatekeeping: helping others to participate; keeping communication channels open; facilitating the participation of others
3. Seeking Information: asking for opinions, facts, feelings	
4. Clarifying: interpreting or elaborating ideas; asking questions in an effort to understand or promote understanding	3. Consensus Testing: asking if a group is nearing a decision; sending up a trial balloon to test a possible conclusion
5. Coordinating/Summarizing: pulling together related ideas; restating suggestions; offering a decision or conclusion for the group to consider	4. Encouraging: being friendly, warm, and responsive to others; indicating (by facial expression or remark) an interest in others' contributions
6. Reality Testing: making a critical analysis of an idea; testing an idea against some data; trying to see if the idea would work	5. Compromising: when one's own idea or status is involved in a conflict, offering a compromise that yields status; modifying in the interest of group cohesion or growth

service departments can provide information, staff, expertise, facilities, and equipment that can be vital to the success of the team.

The effective team builds key relationships with people outside the team. The team leader is usually the person with the responsibility for external relations, but the leader may not always be the best person to handle every contact. Even the person from the same discipline or with the requisite expertise may not be the most appropriate to handle the interface. Managing the "boundary" is an important aspect of teamwork, and selecting the best person is the key decision. For example, teams may elect to have a person who lacks the technical expertise but who possesses high-level negotiating skills to manage the budget process and good communications skills to facilitate a users' meeting.

Managing the "outside" often involves the creation of a positive image. Teams find that doing a good job is not enough; they must find ways to communicate their successes to significant others on the invisible team. Many teams create a newsletter, others resort to presentations at meetings, and still others focus on personal contact by team members. Lack of information about the team can lead to a lack of credibility. Ultimately, poor image can hamper success.

External relations also involve building a network of contacts who can assist the team. This network can help the team get an approval quickly through the bureaucracy, obtain funds for a special project, locate an expert to solve a team problem, smooth out a conflict with another organization, or find new product and service ideas.

All of this network building is geared to the mobilization of resources. Teams need help, and the effective teams get the resources they need when they need them. Effective teams lay the groundwork by building a positive image, confidence, and active support for their efforts.

Building support for a team is especially crucial for a new team or for a team with a new idea. It is important for members to be "engaged in a process of informing others, understanding and overcoming their objections, understanding the factions and motives of the different parties involved, lobbying and persuading these key figures how the idea can benefit the organization" (Hastings, Bixby, and Chaudhry-Lawton, 1987, p. 49).

The result of this networking can be some fascinating interpersonal dynamics. Effective teams are often seen as a "pain in the butt." The use of this phrase implies both good-natured kidding and healthy respect. Sponsors, customers, and others would sometimes just as soon avoid dealing with the team but are often impressed with the team's fervor and tenacity.

Effective image building with the invisible team also has a salutary effect on team members. As Hastings and his associates (p. 50) note, "[effective] publicity breeds pride and pride reinforces commitment."

Team players help the team build effective external relations by:

- Completing all work assignments in their functional department

- Sharing the credit for team successes with members of the invisible team
- Informing members of the invisible team of important actions that may impact their interactions with the team
- Encouraging honest feedback from clients, customers, and sponsors

Style Diversity. Most of the thinking and writing about teamwork has focused on the group dynamics of an effective team and on management and leadership skills. Very little attention has been given to the composition of the team as a determinant of success or to the concept of *team player*.

My research indicates a variety of ways a person can contribute to a team's success. The next chapter will present a detailed description of the various team-player styles—indications of the many ways members can be helpful to their team. Equally important is the finding that the most successful teams are composed of members who exhibit a diversity of styles. This finding means that a team increases its chances for success if it includes a mix of members who are concerned about high-quality task accomplishment, push the team to set goals and objectives, work hard to ensure a positive team process, and raise questions about the team's operations.

The team of health professionals with the role conflicts we discussed earlier in this chapter also had a diversity of team-player styles. The team consisted of four people. When they completed the Team-Player Survey (see Resource C), the results revealed that each member's primary style was different from those of the other team members. In effect, the team had a "perfect" distribution of the styles—four members, four different styles. The team was composed of one task-focused member, one goal-directed member, one process-oriented member, and one member who questioned the team's methods. When the results were shared, team members recognized two things: (1) how the style differences had reinforced the role conflicts and (2) how the style differences strengthened the team.

We have seen the effects of teams without style diversity. For example, one team of systems developers seemed very busy. In fact, they did work very hard, spending long hours and weekends on their project. They were very bright and set high standards for their work, and they expected high quality from their colleagues. But then, at a project meeting, the frustration that had been building surfaced in an avalanche of self-criticism:

- "We've lost sight of the big picture."
- "This isn't fun anymore."
- "I'm not sure we're doing things right."
- "Are we all in agreement on where we want to be by the end of the year?"

With some help, they began to see their team as being task oriented to the exclusion of other styles. Members of the team were encouraged to expand their repertoire (1) to emphasize the big picture—specifically, to focus on where the project was going and where it fit into other organization efforts in the systems area, (2) to take the time to address the process needs of the team—specifically, to emphasize interpersonal relationships among team members, and (3) regularly to take a hard look at project outcomes and team effectiveness.

By the way, it is quite easy and almost natural for teams to be composed of members with similar orientations. When a team is being organized or when new members are added to an existing team, we look for variety in knowledge and skills to match the team's function. However, when it comes to deciding which engineer or computer programmer we will select, we look for similarity, not diversity. We look for "someone who will fit in," "my kind of guy," "a person who thinks the way we do," or "someone I can relate to."

People simply feel more comfortable around other people with similar styles. It is an effort to appreciate another person with a different way of getting things done. And yet, we know that diversity in both substance and style strengthens a team. Chapter Seven provides guidelines for analyzing your team's strengths and weaknesses and for developing strategies for improvement.

Self-Assessment. Periodically, teams should stop to examine how well they are functioning and what may be interfering with their effectiveness. This self-assessment may be formal or informal. Infor-

mal assessments may take the form of a team member simply asking, "How are we doing?" A good group discussion can be a quick
and effective exercise for a team. Some good questions for such an
exercise are the following: What are our strengths? What are we
doing well? What things should we stop doing because they are
reducing our effectiveness? What should we begin doing that would
increase our effectiveness? Or, to simplify matters even more, we
could just ask, "How can we improve our team?"

An assessment can have more structure and depth, as we see in
the Team-Development Survey (see Resource A). This form uses our
twelve team characteristics as the criteria against which the team is
evaluated. Team players have a variety of applications at their
disposal:

1.   Each team member completes the form. One member receives
     the forms and prepares a summary for presentation and discus-
     sion at a team meeting.
2.   The form is completed at the end of a team meeting. A group
     discussion on each of the items follows.
3.   An outside facilitator interviews each team member using the
     form as a basis for the discussion. The facilitator summarizes
     the results, presents the findings at a team meeting, and leads
     a discussion on increasing team effectiveness.

The Ineffective Team

Poorly functioning teams are not just the mirror image of effective
teams. A team may rank high on some of the dimensions but may
not be addressing several critical areas. The stage of development
determines the critical needs of the team, and if those needs are not
met, the team will not be successful.

For example, in the early stages, a team needs direction and agreement on mission and goals. Therefore, while there may be an informal climate, open communication, and good listening among
members, the team will still be considered ineffective if it lacks a clear
mission and clear goals. In a later stage when conflicts arise, a set of
goals buttressed by hard-working, task-oriented members may not be
sufficient. The team may fail because they lack good process skills to

successfully resolve differences among the members. (See Chapter Six for a description of the stages of team development and what team players can do to adapt successfully to each stage.) A number of warning signs indicate the potential for team difficulties.

Signs of Trouble

You Cannot Easily Describe the Team's Mission. Describing the mission is especially important in the early stages of a team's history. However, it also may be a problem when the team has been together for many years and they have lost their focus. One other test: if you can come up with a mission statement, would other team members agree with you?

The Meetings Are Formal, Stuffy, or Tense. People do not do their best work in an uncomfortable atmosphere. While people may be somewhat reserved during the first few meetings as they assess the situation, be wary if things do not relax after a reasonable period of time. And you might ask yourself whether anyone on the team is making an effort to develop an informal climate.

There Is a Great Deal of Participation but Little Accomplishment. Some teams exhibit a lot of talk but not much action; they simply seem to enjoy the interaction that a group provides. If you are a member of a team that has a high level of involvement, ask yourself whether you are satisfied with the amount of tangible output or progress toward goals in the last three weeks.

There Is Talk but Not Much Communication. Many teams are composed of very talented people who enjoy talking but do not listen to the contributions of others. Listening is the key to effective planning, problem solving, conflict resolution, and decision making. Think about your last team meeting. Did you notice team members asking questions for clarification, paraphrasing to ensure understanding, or summarizing other members' ideas?

Disagreements Are Aired in Private Conversations After the Meeting. Although occasionally there are flare-ups in public, rarely are organizational differences brought out into the open. Healthy teams have open discussions of professional differences. Reflect for a moment. Are you aware of important differences among team members that are not being openly addressed?

Decisions Tend to Be Made by the Formal Leader with Little Meaningful Involvement of Other Team Members. Since many modern managers are aware of the emphasis on participation, there is a greater use today of meetings, surveys, and other methods to obtain team-member involvement in decision making. However, the real test is whether important team discussions and everyone's ideas are seriously considered in an effort to reach a true consensus.

Members Are Not Open with Each Other Because Trust Is Low. In the early stages, a low level of trust is expected as members get to know each other. However, if your team has been together for some time, it would be appropriate to ask whether you feel comfortable airing your true feelings about issues that come up.

There Is Confusion or Disagreement About Roles or Work Assignments. Conflicts usually surface as interpersonal, emotional issues. In other words, people are just plain mad because another team member has done something or failed to do something. Role conflicts are difficult to see. It may require you to sit down with the other team members and ask whether all members think and act as if it is "our" team.

People in Other Parts of the Organization Who Are Critical to the Success of the Team Are Not Cooperating. Teams usually require the assistance of external people who provide funds, equipment, staff, and intangible support. There is rarely a period in a team's history when good external relations are not important. At any point, it would be important to ask whether there are significant people out there who do not know what we are doing or who are aware of our work but are not supportive.

The Team Is Overloaded with People Who Have the Same Team-Player Style. While there may be diversity in technical expertise, there is often a similarity in approach to teamwork. Style diversity leads to looking at all aspects of team effectiveness. If you suspect a lack of style diversity on your team, consider whether members are equally concerned about completing tasks in a highly professional manner, setting goals and ensuring all work is directed toward those goals, developing and maintaining the group as a team, and candidly questioning goals and methods.

The Team Has Been in Existence for at Least Three Months and Has Never Assessed Its Functioning. Periodically, teams need to assess progress toward goals and to evaluate team process. Look around at your team and ask, "When was the last time we took a hard look at ourselves?"

Building Your Team

The first step in the process of increasing the effectiveness of your team is to assess the current state of the team. The twelve dimensions of team effectiveness provide the framework, and the Team-Development Survey, found in Resource A, provides the vehicle.

Prior to the administration of the survey, the team should review each of the twelve characteristics to arrive at an understanding of the meaning of each item in the context of your team. Bring the framework to life by asking questions: How would effective listening skills help us? What would open communication look like on our team? What are the roles played by members of our team?

When the survey is distributed, team members should be asked to provide examples to explain their ratings. These examples will add meaning to the discussion and provide the basis for an improvement plan.

Team members should be asked to share these responses and to discuss the reasons for their answers. Here is where the examples will be helpful. You will find that the discussion of the results will reflect many of the issues included in the survey (listening, open communication, civilized disagreement, consensus decisions). For example, when analyzing the survey results, are we using good listening skills?

Finally, this exercise should lead to an identification of your strengths as a team. It is important to highlight these areas and then to look for ways to support them in the future. Weaknesses also should be identified, followed by analysis and development of an action plan to improve each area.

Team development requires taking a hard look at the current effectiveness of your organization. Our twelve characteristics provide a framework to direct the effort.

The effective team is equally concerned with getting the job done and how the job gets done—both the means and the end. A team needs to think strategically about the future and about its role in the organization. At the same time, the effective team is building and maintaining a positive internal climate.

Effective teams require effective team players. Each of the dimensions of the effective team is furthered by the actions of effective team players. In the next chapter, the characteristics of the effective team player are described and linked to the success of the team.

Chapter Three

Effective Team Players

A team player isn't an isolated example. It's a way of life that is exhibited in everything they do—including others in decisions, sharing, pitching in, networking, looking for new ways of doing things, etc.
                    —Kathy Zarr, Northwestern Mutual Life.*

Being a team player is a way of life. There are many ways that people in organizations can contribute to the success of a team, but in the past we have had a limited, often one-dimensional view of the team player.

In sports, the team player throws the great block that allows the halfback to score the winning touchdown, makes the beautiful pass that leads to the important basket, or "plays hurt" in the championship game.

In business, the team player supports the company program without making waves, does the behind-the-scenes work necessary for the big presentation, or drives through a snowstorm to make a delivery to a customer.

We now know that teamwork and being a team player are more complex. The project teams at Chrysler who are designing and manufacturing new models, the drug development teams at Merck who are bringing new compounds to market, the research and development teams at Calgon and Coors who are reducing the time it takes to commercialize a new product all require a rich combination of the dimensions of effective teamwork. Although all of the elements are not present in every case, a few characteristics stand out:

*Survey response.

61

- A clear mission and plan to accomplish it
- Positive relationships with and support from other parts of the organization
- Excellent communication, openness, and trust among team members
- A blend of people, each contributing a special talent

Teamwork requires team players. Effective teamwork is based upon an effective mix of people who exhibit a variety of styles or approaches to teamwork. In our description of the characteristics of an effective team, we called this *style diversity*. In this chapter, we will explore the various styles in some detail.

The Concept of Personal Style

Anyone who thinks about the concept of styles owes an intellectual debt to the psychological theorist Carl Jung. Jung wanted to demystify psychology and create a practical approach to the description of individuals. Jung (1923) called them *psychological types*. Jung's types result from a combination of two attitudes—introversion and extroversion—and four functions—(1) thinking, (2) feeling, (3) sensation, and (4) intuition.

Jung combined the attitudes and functions and created eight psychological types. Although it is not important to describe Jung's types in detail, it is significant to note how he saw the types manifesting themselves in the real world. Jung's principles provide a useful backdrop for the application of our team-player styles:

1. The types are categories in which people with similar but not necessarily the same characteristics are found.
2. A person may exhibit one type in one situation and another type in another situation, but he or she usually has one type that predominates in most situations.
3. Each person has the capacity to exhibit all types. In other words, none of the attitudes and functions is missing from anyone.
4. A person's unique combination of characteristics that identify him or her as a particular type is subject to change. Jung be-

lieved that the pressures to change were external (parents, society), but we have come to believe changes can be self-directed.

The Myers-Briggs Type Indicator (MBTI) is an instrument used to classify people according to Jungian types (Briggs and Myers, 1957). The MBTI has been extensively validated and is widely used. However, since it was developed primarily as an aid in counseling, it has not been as useful in management and team development. Many other style instruments have been developed for use in organizational settings. They focus on styles of decision making, leadership, and interpersonal relationships (Rowe and Mason, 1987; Atkins, 1981). But no research-based instruments focus on team-player styles.

Team-Player Styles

Our research indicates four types or styles of team players. Each style contributes in different ways to the success of the team, and each style has a downside when carried to an extreme, as we shall see in the next chapter.

Each of us has the capacity to be an effective team player but in different ways. You and I both can be positive contributors to a team and yet act in very different fashions. For example, you may be willing to learn a new system and take on an added responsibility that is needed by the team. I may help by encouraging some of the quiet people to get involved in the discussions or by using humor to reduce conflicts in the group. Another team member may recommend that we develop goals and an action plan, and someone else may insist that we take a critical look at one of our pet projects.

We begin the discussion of the four team-player styles by presenting a brief summary of each one. The brief style summaries are followed by detailed descriptions. As you review the characteristics that describe each style, think about your primary team at work. Which of these descriptions best identifies your primary style? Which descriptions best fit your colleagues?

A *Contributor* is a task-oriented team member who enjoys providing the team with good technical information and data, does his or her homework, and pushes the team to set high performance standards and to use their resources wisely. Most people see the Contributor as dependable.

A *Collaborator* is a goal-directed member who sees the vision, mission, or goal of the team as paramount but is flexible and open to new ideas, is willing to pitch in and work outside his or her defined role, and is able to share the limelight with other team members. Most people see the Collaborator as a "big-picture" person.

A *Communicator* is a process-oriented member who is an effective listener and facilitator of involvement, conflict resolution, consensus building, feedback, and the building of an informal, relaxed climate. Most people see the Communicator as a positive people person.

A *Challenger* is a member who questions the goals, methods, and even the ethics of the team, is willing to disagree with the leader or higher authority, and encourages the team to take well-conceived risks. Most people appreciate the value of the Challenger's candor and openness.

Contributor

A task-oriented team member, the Contributor sees his or her role as providing the group with the best possible information. In the Contributor's view, effective team problem solving and decision making result from the sharing of team members' expertise. The Contributor sees a team as a group of subject-matter experts who are expected to complete a series of task assignments. The success of the team is determined by (1) a strong leader who ensures that tasks are distributed among team members and (2) members who finish their assignments in a timely and complete fashion.

Contributors help their teams by freely offering all the relevant knowledge, skills, and data they possess. They realize they are members of the team because they have certain information about the business or about a functional area—information they are expected to contribute. The complex nature of many businesses today requires the use of cross-functional teams to solve problems and meet customer needs. At Digital Equipment Corporation (DEC), cross-functional teams work together to provide customers with in-

Figure 1. Four Team-Player Styles.

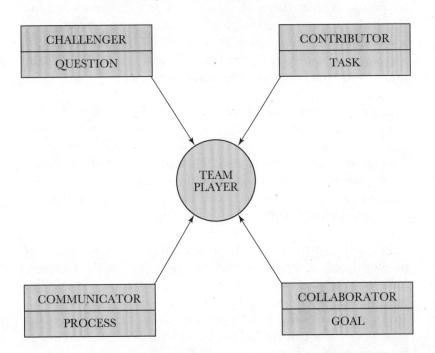

tegrated solutions; at Merck and Company, multidisciplinary teams come together to develop new drugs. Effective Contributors are critical to the success of these teams. As Anne Rarich of DEC puts it, "Team players know their own business and that of other key players in other parts of the company who will make things happen."

Freely sharing their expertise means that they do not hold back or hoard information. In some competitive environments, team players withhold technical knowledge from their colleagues because they fear a loss of an "edge" in annual performance appraisals. Some corporate cultures foster this dysfunctional behavior by pitting employees against each other, although some people bring this competitive, antiteamwork mentality to the workplace themselves. There are specific strategies for addressing this organizational problem. They will be outlined in Chapter Eight.

The sharing of information by the Contributor is expressed in a number of positive ways. A number of our survey respondents pointed to the teaching or training of other team members as an important characteristic of a team player. Cummins Engine Company's Charles Chasteen puts "training new team members" in a manufacturing environment at the top of the list. Victor Kline, in response to our survey, reported this vignette of an effective team player at McNeil Consumer Products Company:

> A line manager volunteered to serve as an instructor for a quality education workshop. He ordered and assembled the training materials, arrived at class early to help set up and volunteered to stay late to assist. He kept all his commitments, maintained an up-beat attitude throughout and, after the course, sent his fellow instructors memos telling them what a nice job they did, with copies sent to their bosses.

People's expertise is usually the main reason they are hired and promoted and, generally, is why they are valued in the company. It is how they are known. It is what sets them apart from other people in the organization. Therefore, to share the very thing that determines your value is to make a significant contribution as a team player. For this reason, the Contributor's role as a trainer or mentor is highly valued.

The sharing dimension of the contributory team player is seen in the diligence with which all team assignments are completed. The Contributor is someone who sees assignments to collect data, conduct studies, and prepare reports as obligations to be met. Contributors attack these tasks with intensity because they see them as their major opportunities to be positive team players. They believe that successful task completion is the key to a successful team. In fact, they often become impatient with other team members who do not approach their assignments with the same fervor.

There are some downside risks to this aspect of the Contributor. For example, Merrill Lynch Relocation Management's David Gilman sees a team player as "giving up one's own time and resources to assist others without any direct 'what's in it for me' attitude, *while still completing their own work*." There will be negative implications, Gilman points out in his survey response, if Contributors do not complete their regular responsibilities while they are assisting other people. The other people in the work area who must complete the unfinished tasks of the Contributors become resentful. This is especially true if the Contributors are being lauded by others as being "outstanding team players."

Effective team players contribute to their teams, but they also complete all work in the regular job area. They do not use their team tasks as an excuse to sidestep functional work assignments. This conduct is especially important in companies that make heavy use of cross-functional teams or in matrix organizations. Balancing the team's need for data to solve problems with the department's need to have its work completed is a tricky but important trait of a successful Contributor.

Effective team players have a clear sense of priorities. They know and are able to rank the myriad of tasks before them. Since, as David Gilman points out, "Team players usually do not say 'no' to requests," they are able to prioritize those requests. In addition, they set realistic deadlines for their deliverables. The Contributor hates to disappoint the other team members and, therefore, sometimes experiences difficulties serving the needs of two organizations. When conflicts exist, the Contributor looks to the team leader to provide direction in regard to the relative importance of the various projects. The Contributor has a low tolerance for ambiguity and will make a priority decision if no direction is provided by the leader.

During the 1940s and 1950s, a New York Yankees baseball player, Tommy Hendrick, was called "Old Reliable" by his teammates. Hendrick seemed to do what was necessary to win the game—make a great catch in a critical situation or hit a home run in the bottom of the ninth inning. He was dependable. And that same adjective is often used to describe effective team players. They are the people the team turns to when quality and timeliness are important. The Contributor does not let the team down.

The manner in which information is shared is equally important. The Contributor takes great care to prepare the information he or she presents to the team. No last-minute, slipshod, handwritten, unedited reports from this person. The Contributor's presentations—oral or written—are professionally prepared and delivered. Contributors invest great effort in the project, and they invest equally in the presentation because they want their colleagues to give serious consideration to their work.

Contributors set high personal standards for work and push the team to establish and live up to superior measures. They use words like *quality* and *excellence* and *results* to describe their expectations. Contributors have low tolerance for shortcuts in research, compromises in quality, and incomplete data. They believe their work is thorough and complete, and they insist that other team members hold to the same high standards. Professionalism is highly valued by the Contributor.

Given the emphasis on high standards, it is not surprising that the Contributor believes strongly in what Charles Chasteen, in his response to our survey, calls "accepting responsibility for one's actions and their consequences." What Chasteen has in mind is standing up and being held accountable. The team concept sometimes allows people to hide in the shadow of others when problems arise, when deadlines are missed, and when results are questioned. Contributory team players expect to take responsibility for their work and to answer to their colleagues for the results of their efforts. And they expect the same standard to be applied to all members of the team. In fact, Contributors are likely to initiate accountability discussions when their work is under consideration.

Contributors also value efficiency. Team efficiency means judicious use of time and resources. Everyone is concerned about wasting time, but the Contributor will insist that the team make a special effort to minimize the amount of time spent in meetings and to optimize the time allocated to those meetings. They push the team to establish a well-thought-out agenda (including time allocations), to limit the length of presentations, to encourage the use of subcommittees, and to recommend methods other than meetings (such as electronic mail) for communicating information.

Contributor: A Summary

Contributors provide the team with the valuable technical expertise it needs to solve problems and meet its goals. They provide the data and they provide it in a manner in which it can be easily used. And they often serve as trainers and mentors of other team members.

They help the team set high standards, define priorities, and make efficient use of team meeting time and resources.

Contributor: A Checklist of Behaviors

1. Freely shares all relevant information and opinions with other team members
2. Helps the team use its time and resources
3. Pushes the team to set high standards and to achieve top-level results and insists on high-quality outputs
4. Completes all team assignments and other relevant homework necessary for the completion of team tasks
5. Accepts responsibility for all actions as a team member
6. Completes all work in his or her regular job area and all other tasks not related to the team
7. Provides the team with clear, concise, and useful presentations at team meetings
8. Provides technical training for other team members and serves as a mentor for new team members
9. Has a clear set of priorities

Contributor: A Checklist of Adjectives

1. Dependable
2. Responsible
3. Organized
4. Efficient
5. Logical
6. Clear
7. Relevant
8. Pragmatic
9. Systematic
10. Proficient

Collaborator

A goal-directed player, the Collaborator sees the vision, goal, or current task as paramount in all interactions. The Collaborator is constantly reminding the team to stay on track and to make sure everything is focused on the target—bringing the drug to market, completing the new system on time, or meeting the production schedule.

Collaborators are willing to work outside their defined roles to get the work done. They never say, "That's not my job," or "My boss won't approve it." In his response to our survey, Bill McClung of Johnson & Johnson Baby Products says he sees team players as having the "ability and willingness to do work that will benefit the team effort that is outside their area of expertise." McClung cites the example of a new product team that worked all night loading trucks with product to meet a test-market deadline.

"Pitching in" is a phrase many people use to describe the collaborative team player. Examples abound:

- The bank branch manager who opens a teller's window when the lines are long
- The vice-president of personnel who is collating manuals the night before the launch of a new training program
- The analyst who cancelled a vacation because she got a telephone call about a system problem the night before her scheduled departure

Sue Ogle of People's Bank in Bridgeport, Connecticut, says it very directly in her response to our survey: "Team players pitch in and help others when they need assistance." Organization development consultant and author of *The Empowered Manager* (1987), Peter Block, in his survey response, simply says, "They cover for each other."

Linked with a willingness to pitch in is the willingness to share the limelight, a characteristic repeatedly cited by our survey respondents. One respondent, Gordon Luce, chairman and CEO of Great American First Savings Bank, reported on "a major investment with great results which was conceived by one executive but he shared the congratulations and results with a committee of team players who got equal credit."

Sharing the limelight may mean working behind the scenes—in effect, not getting any "light" at all. Team players may do the data collection, report writing, speech drafting, preparation of the visuals for a presentation, logistics, and a myriad of other things required for accomplishment of a team's task. Collaborative people regularly perform in this fashion.

"Team players can set aside their own egos when necessary" is the way Dave Leeper of Bell Communications Research puts it. Team players derive satisfaction from being part of a successful team rather than just being good individual contributors. They realize their contributions are necessary for the team's success, but they do not require individual recognition to be satisfied with the work.

All of this behavior suggests a commitment to team goals. When asked to rank a list of team-player characteristics, our survey respondents put "commitment to team goals" at the top of the list. In the course of many training workshops, we have asked participants to rank a similar list, and each time the "commitment" characteristic is selected as number one. Ken Ewing of Hershey Chocolate Company is very much to the point when he says in response to our survey, "Team players focus on what's good for the business not just what's good for me and my department."

This commitment requires a necessary first step and therefore the need to back up before we go forward. Too many teams do not take the time to work through the goal-setting process. Collaborative team players, however, insist that their team establish a clear mission or charter before proceeding with the work. A mission specifies your products or services and your customers. In other words, it answers the questions "What do you do?" and "For whom do you do it?" And it is important to understand that a mission is not something just for the top of the house. Every division, department, committee, task force, or other business team should have a clear mission, a reason for being.

Collaborators then help the team develop a set of long-range goals and short-term objectives. They want to be part of an organization that is going somewhere—an organization that has a sense of direction and a plan to get there. When required, they may be visionary as well. That is, they encourage the team to take a strategic view—to think about the future, to create what Warren Bennis (1989, p. 20) refers to as a "sense of outcome, goal, or direction" for the organization. Collaborators are uncomfortable with teams that see goal setting as the development of a "to-do" list for the next year. They express their discomfort by insisting on a period of time for goal-stretching exercises.

The Collaborator also brings the goal-setting process to the daily environment. While the big picture is important, the current task is also significant. The collaborative team player helps the team understand and clarify its immediate work assignment and its reason for meeting. Questions such as "What's our purpose for meeting today?" and "What do we hope to accomplish?" and, even more basic, "What is the agenda?" help the team move forward in a systematic fashion. At a recent team meeting, the chairperson of a task force seemed poorly prepared for the session. Another member, playing the Collaborator role, got the meeting moving by pulling out the milestone chart and identifying the task assignments that were due that day.

Once vision, mission, goals, objectives, and plans are in place, effective teams take the time to revisit them on a regular basis. Plans may be reviewed daily, weekly, or monthly; objectives should be reviewed monthly or quarterly; and at an annual meeting, teams should assess progress toward goals. The ongoing validity of the mission and vision also may be examined on an annual basis. Collaborators remind the team and even insist that these reviews take place. They know that without periodic reviews, the goal-setting process loses credibility and, even more important, the inherent value of goal setting is lost to the team.

Committed team players will work toward goals or will complete specific tasks even though they may not agree with them. It is easy to push ahead toward team goals that are aligned with your personal goals or values. However, a litmus test for a real team player is the willingness to work in earnest for a goal that was approved over his or her objections. At Wang Laboratories, six vice-presidents worked together to build a three-year strategy for the manufacturing division and, as Dick Kropp, director of human resources, notes in his survey response, "They all knew going in that the outcome would result in some of them losing a piece of their turf and yet they proceeded to work toward implementation."

Closely related to the capability to support all team goals is the need to support the team in all interactions outside the team. Positive team players will argue their points with intensity during the meeting but, win or lose, they will support the outcome. The negative team players will bad-mouth the work of the team and often reveal the details of discussions, intending to embarrass other team members. In the end, the whole team loses because the image of the team is tarnished. As Peter Block, in his response to our survey, puts it, "On effective teams there is a lack of gossip and sabotage." Collaborative team players speak with pride and enthusiasm about their team.

Collaborators also see the big picture and help the team see how their goals fit with some larger context. As Warren Bennis (1988) reminds us, "Text without context is pretext." The environment, the organization, and the culture in which a team functions have fundamental impacts on success. Collaborators play the role of the team player who regularly reminds the team of where they fit and of the importance of positive interactions with significant players. For most teams, there is a need to manage effectively the interface with other units within the same organization, with customers, and often with regulatory agencies.

The Collaborator is open to new ideas and data even when that information may suggest an alteration of team goals and plans. In our survey, "openness to new ideas" was one of the three most frequently mentioned characteristics of an effective team player. In his response to our survey, Floyd Whellan, vice-president of human resources for Lee Enterprises, a chain of newspaper and television stations, sees a team player as someone who "recognizes the importance of having ideas contributed from various sources and is willing to have an 'open window' and permit those ideas to impact their behavior." In addition, Whellan finds team players to be less rigid and, as a result, more creative and innovative.

When asked for a specific example of a team player, Dale Dunn of ARCO Oil and Gas Company pointed to a vice-president who surveyed department employees requesting input on ways to increase effectiveness in the areas of communications, goals, and other organizational issues. He scheduled meetings to discuss the survey results and followed up on all suggestions and changes.

At the personal level, the effective Collaborator is open to hearing and doing something about critical feedback. The openness extends to his or her own behavior as a team member. This open posture is typically the outgrowth of a high level of self-esteem. Many people in our survey saw effective team players as secure, confident people who usually feel good about themselves. This characteristic seems to be a necessary condition for openness and for a willingness to change—both organizationally and interpersonally.

Collaborator: A Summary

Collaborators play a key role in keeping a team goal directed and focused on the steps necessary to reach that goal. They serve as models by working outside their prescribed jobs and being willing to spread around the kudos of team success. In a pinch, they will drop everything to help out other team members. They are open to new ideas that may impact the team's efforts and to feedback about their own performance.

Collaborator: A Checklist of Behaviors

1. Helps the team establish long-term goals and clarify its current objective or task
2. Helps the team see how its work fits into the total organization
3. Regularly reminds the team of the need to revisit their goals and action plans
4. Encourages the team to establish plans with milestones and appropriate task assignments
5. Pitches in to help out other team members who need assistance
6. Works hard to achieve team goals and to complete the current tasks even though he or she may not agree with them
7. Does not gossip about other team members or share negative comments about team process with nonmembers
8. Is flexible and open to new ideas or data that may alter team goals

9.   Often works outside his or her defined role to help the team achieve its goals
10.   Is willing to share the limelight with other team members

Collaborator: A Checklist of Adjectives

1.   Cooperative
2.   Flexible
3.   Confident
4.   Forward-looking
5.   Conceptual
6.   Accommodating
7.   Generous
8.   Open
9.   Visionary
10.   Imaginative

Communicator

The Communicator gives primary emphasis to team process—how the team goes about completing its tasks and reaching its goals. The Communicator believes there is an interpersonal "glue" that must be present for a team to be effective. Although the Communicator's efforts are sometimes resisted by other members, everyone agrees that teams succeed or fail based upon attention to process issues. Despite the fact that our description of the effective team includes many process dimensions (listening, communication, disagreements), most people would rather not address these subjects. Team goals, roles, and task assignments are easier issues to confront.

We all know that the climate and culture of a team are critical to the success of the total effort. Climate influences such factors as productivity, creativity, and problem solving. The Communicator contributes to a positive climate by helping people on the team get to know and feel comfortable with each other. This does not mean that everyone's deepest and darkest secrets must be revealed. As a participant recently said to me, "I'm a very private person, and I don't like telling other people about my personal life." I indicated that his statement was sufficiently revealing, and we went on to discuss his work life.

The Communicator is especially helpful at the time of team formation—the awkward period when people are waiting for direction. The Communicator is helpful when the composition of the team changes or when a new member joins the team. People simply want to know who the other players are and what they bring to the party. This orientation extends beyond the personal dimension to the skills, resources, and experience each person will contribute to the work of the team. For example, at the first meeting of a major task force, all members detailed the projects they had worked on, the programming languages they knew, and the systems with which they had experience. This information was posted on flip charts around the room, and the net result was the creation of a team talent bank.

The informal climate that was mentioned as a hallmark of the effective team is facilitated by the Communicator. He or she initiates and supports pre- and post-meeting discussions of nonwork subjects (family, vacations, hobbies, sports) that help set a relaxed atmosphere. Good-natured jokes and comments that break the tension or smooth over an awkward moment contribute to the effectiveness of the team. The Communicator uses humor, tact, and even diplomacy to encourage informality and to reduce destructive conflict. As Cathie Black, publisher of *USA Today*, put it, "Humor is a great gift because it is a great weapon. It deflects hostility, tension, anger" (Cohen, 1989, p. 83).

Another key element of a team's success is the ability of team members to listen to each other. The Communicator models this characteristic in many ways. At a recent meeting, a vice-president asked questions to obtain more information or clarification, paraphrased the responses, and took notes on the answers. He sent a simple, direct, and powerful message to the other players on his team.

Effective Communicators listen to the complete story. They do not interrupt presentations or comments by other team members, and often they will caution others to do the same. They work hard to withhold judgment until all the facts and opinions are outlined and the conclusions presented. Good listeners are valued as team members because of what they contribute to positive team process. They are also valued because listening is a skill that is in short supply.

Communicators are not laid-back, laissez-faire participants. They believe, as one of our survey respondents said, "Communication is not a spectator sport." Good Communicators are active. They step in and take an active role when ineffectual process is standing in the way of goal attainment. Communicators encourage quiet members to give their opinions, ask the more talkative people to give other members an opportunity to share their views, request that members confine their disagreements to the subject and eliminate personal attacks, and suggest that the team establish certain norms or guidelines for team interactions.

These interventions can be risky; but like all risks, the payoffs can be great. Another series of risky interventions concerns feedback—both the giving and receiving of comments about behavior as a team player. Effective team players tend to be confident people with a high level of self-esteem. Therefore, they are able to receive feedback about their performance without becoming defensive. As Howard Guttman of Johnson & Johnson's Personal Products Company observed in his survey response, "Team players show a willingness to hear and do something about critical feedback." In fact, they will often initiate a conversation in which they solicit feedback about their performance as team players.

Communicators also offer feedback to other team members about their participation on the team. Effective team players know how to offer comments that are specific, intended to be helpful, and expressed in a manner such that the other person will be able to hear and use it. Feedback is a process that requires skill and courage.

Communicative team players are active in other ways. They project enthusiasm about the team's work, about progress toward the goal, and about accomplishments along the way. They are positive people. For them, the glass is half full rather than half empty. Failures are opportunities to learn. They have, as our survey respondent Jay Wright of AT&T puts it, "a can-do attitude." For Wright, team players are "energy givers rather than energy users." Communicators have the ability to persevere and to spread that energy to other team players. When teams are performing well, the competitive cohesion that develops is usually fostered by the Communicator. Team members feel good about their team, and a friendly competition develops with other teams.

This enthusiasm extends to a sense of urgency about the work of the team. Communicators spur the team to move forward with their work. They are able to establish and maintain a momentum that is necessary to sustain a team over a long period. This sense of movement is extremely important because teams usually experience an ebb and flow that includes periods of great progress mixed with times of slow growth or even retreat. Layoffs, reorganizations, budget cuts, and changing priorities all impact team climate. Teams need key players who will urge them to move ahead during these periods.

Team members need recognition and praise for their efforts, and Communicators have a knack of knowing when to deliver this message. They know that recognition usually costs nothing and, therefore, they are not stingy with it. In a recent survey I conducted for a company, "lack of recognition for performance" was cited as the major employee complaint. People said they wanted some form of recognition beyond salary treatment—from a positive verbal comment to a commendation letter with a copy sent to their supervisors. Communicators are usually ready with a "good job" or a "thanks for the extra effort" at a meeting or with a margin note on a memo or report.

The ongoing praise should be supplemented by larger recognition events when milestones are reached or when significant outcomes are achieved. The Communicator will urge the team to take the time to celebrate their accomplishments and recognize members.

We propose the consensus method as the preferred approach to decision making in certain critical team situations. However, a consensus does not just suddenly emerge because we want it to happen; this is when the Communicator plays a critical role. He or she will encourage participation from everyone, discourage voting, tease out the reasons behind opinions, ask for data or prior experience with the issue, and summarize the key points. The summary may form the basis for a consensus, or it may simply point out the areas of agreement and disagreement. At a certain time, the Communicator will see the basis for consensus and test the waters for possible agreement by saying, for example, "It sounds like most of us agree that customer service is the number-one priority and we should develop a plan for establishing a new customer service department."

Finally, effective team players will recognize the importance of a periodic team self-assessment. They will propose that the team take some time to ask and answer the question "How are we doing?" This review can include a look at progress toward the goals, a check on the milestones, and an evaluation of team process— communication, participation, conflict resolution, and listening. The assessment should conclude with an acknowledgment of successes and a plan for improvement.

Communicator: A Summary

A process-oriented member, the Communicator is an effective listener and facilitator of participation, conflict resolution, consensus building, feedback, and the building of an informal, relaxed climate.

Communicator: A Checklist of Behaviors

1. Steps in to resolve process problems such as conflict among team members or lack of involvement by some members
2. Listens attentively, while withholding judgment, to all viewpoints
3. Helps the team relax and have fun by joking, laughing, and discussing personal interests
4. Recognizes and praises other team members for their efforts
5. Communicates enthusiasm and sense of urgency about the team's work
6. Periodically summarizes the status of a discussion or proposes a possible consensus
7. Encourages other team members to participate in the discussions and decisions of the team
8. Helps the people on the team get to know each other and to know what skills and resources each can contribute
9. Gives feedback to other team members—feedback that is descriptive, specific, and intended to be helpful

10. Receives feedback from other team members without becoming defensive
11. Reminds the team to take the time periodically to assess team effectiveness and plan for improvement

Communicator: A Checklist of Adjectives

1. Supportive
2. Encouraging
3. Relaxed
4. Tactful
5. Helpful
6. Friendly
7. Patient
8. Informal
9. Considerate
10. Spontaneous

Challenger

A colleague told me the following story about a management board meeting of a bank: "At one point during the meeting, the president asked, 'How's morale around here?' The first person to respond was the vice-president sitting to the left of the president. He said that on a scale of 10 he would rate morale an 8. The remainder of the vice-presidents responded with a 7 or 8. When my turn came, I wanted to tell the truth and say 3 or 4 but I didn't have the courage."

This story illustrates groupthink at its worst. It may be that the vice-presidents believed the president did not want to hear bad news and, therefore, simply were being good soldiers. In other words, the climate did not support honesty, especially when it required the delivery of unpleasant information. Nevertheless, effective teamwork requires people who will speak out with an honest and authentic voice. This is the role of the Challenger.

Challengers, as one person in our survey reported, are willing to "swim against the tide." They are candid, open, honest, and, above all, deeply concerned about the direction of the team. And they very much want the team to succeed. However, Challengers may appear to be a negative force on the team since they express opposition to the prevailing thinking and even to the team leader. But the effective Challenger opposes team direction with good intentions, not merely to be against something.

One key test for the Challenger is the ability to speak out, as in the bank example cited above, even when his or her views are contrary to the vast majority of the team. Speaking out is an indication of a team player's strength because the culture of most organizations discourages the expression of minority views. In fact, antiestablishment thoughts are considered the very antithesis of team-player behavior. As a result of interviews with 100 managers in two companies, Robert Jackall (1983, p. 123) found that, "While being a team player has many meanings, one of the most important is to be interchangeable with other managers near one's level. Corporations discourage narrow specialization more strongly as one goes higher. They also *discourage the expression of moral or political qualms.* . . . The public statement of such objection would end any realistic aspirations for higher posts because one's usefulness to the organization depends on versatility" (emphasis added).

Ironically, many Challengers are accused of not being team players because they raise objections to team decisions. If the corporate norm about teamwork is "To get along, go along," then the Challenger will not be accepted as a team player. However, in that kind of culture, being accused of not being a team player is a sure sign of a courageous Challenger.

Disagreeing with the team leader is one of the most difficult acts for the Challenger. It is difficult because the leader is by definition in a position of authority and often is higher in the official corporate hierarchy as well. As one person said to me when I suggested that he say something to the chairperson about a problem, "Are you crazy? She's got too many Hay points!" However, at a meeting at another company a few weeks later, I saw a team member challenge a position taken by the chairperson. The chairperson reacted well to the comment, suggesting that it was a view he had not considered. The impact on the other team members was dramatic. It freed them to increase both the quality and depth of their participation. Honesty is potent.

The Challenger will also raise questions about the team's fundamental mission and goals. At management meetings at a major computer company, I have heard team members voice their strong opposition to the corporate goal of becoming a key player in the personal computer market. This was a brave act because the decision to proceed had been made at the top of the house. As survey respondent Floyd Whellan of Lee Enterprises pointed out to me, "A team player must be willing to speak out when the corporation may be making a decision which may appear to be correct but in principle is inconsistent with our long-term goals."

At team meetings, the challenging team player will not be reluctant to ask pointed questions about reports and presentations. A Challenger wants to know

1. Why certain things are being done
2. If alternatives have been considered
3. The costs versus the benefits
4. The impacts on customers
5. How employees will be affected
6. Whether something can be tried out on a pilot basis

Often the Challenger will make other team members feel uncomfortable. The questions and disagreements may point out lack of preparation, failure to review a problem thoroughly, or questionable integrity. While almost everyone would agree intellectually with the need for these issues to be raised, in practice, many members probably wish the Challenger would just go away. As one person said to me in describing a Challenger in his company, "He's really a pain in the butt." In fact, many Challengers are stereotyped as the iconoclast or resident weirdo. But for many people, "honest and authentic" is the best way to describe the Challenger. As team players, they are factual and truthful in reporting results, and they expect other members to be the same. They are also open about problems facing the team—including their own contributions. Challengers push the team to talk openly about quality problems, budget overruns, customer complaints, employee dissatisfaction, and missed deadlines.

Closely aligned with the need for open discussion of team progress and problems is the need for maintaining the confidentiality of the discussions. The Challenger, like the Collaborator, believes that these discussions should not be the subject of gossip and loose talk outside of team meetings. Strict ground rules regarding frank deliberations need to be established so team members will feel free to be open and candid.

The Challenger is a highly ethical person who encourages the team to set high ethical standards for their work. He or she will insist that the team behave as follows:

- Be truthful, sincere and forthright and not lie, cheat or deceive
- Be honorable, principled and courageous and not adopt an end justifies the means philosophy
- Keep promises, fulfill commitments, and not interpret agreements in an overly technical or legalistic manner in order to escape compliance
- Be open-minded, treat people equally, tolerate diversity and not take unfair advantage of another person's difficulties
- Accept responsibility for their decisions and the consequences of their activities ["Ethical Values and Principles," 1988, p. 153].

Once again, insistence on high ethical standards does raise the discomfort level of some other team members. This is the role of the Challenger.

Pushed to the extreme, the Challenger becomes a whistle-blower who will go public with illegal and unethical team actions. The effective Challenger will be a good team player and try to resolve the issue in the context of the team or with the leadership of the team. In other words, Challengers will exhaust all internal avenues of negotiation before taking the issue to an outside forum. And they will remain ethical in their pursuit of the issue. They will not bring charges against the team to obtain publicity, to settle a grudge, or in some other way to gain personally from their actions. In fact, just the reverse is likely to result. They may lose their jobs and be branded as troublemakers.

One of the most famous Challengers in recent years was Jerome

J. LiCari, director of research and development at Beechnut Nutri-
tion Corporation. LiCari discovered that the apple juice concentrate
sold to Beechnut by a supplier contained little or no juice. Beechnut
was selling the apple juice for babies as "100% fruit juice with no
sugar added." Via memos, reports, and meetings with his superiors,
LiCari tried for four years to get the company to act on the evidence.
At one point, LiCari's supervisor told him that he was not being
a team player and threatened that if he continued to pursue this
issue, he would be fired. Finally, in 1982, some four years after he
first discovered the adulterated concentrate, he resigned. Ultimately,
two Beechnut executives were convicted of selling the bogus product, sentenced to one year in jail, and each fined $100,000. The
company was fined $2 million. The company also settled a civil suit
in the amount of $7.5 million (Traub, 1988).

Challengers will also push the team to be more creative in their
problem solving. Challengers encourage their team not to be bound
by the past or other restrictions but to use brainstorming to get a
free flow of new ideas. They will ask the team to set aside the "killer
phrases" that stifle creativity:

- "We tried that last year."
- "Our boss won't buy it."
- "It's not in the budget."
- "That's not our job."

Effective team players cringe when they hear these phrases and
will challenge the team to override these objections or, better still,
not to raise or discuss them until the ideation stage is complete.
"Let the good ideas flow" is the theme of the Challengers. They
know that climates that encourage risk taking are necessary for real
innovation to take place. Challenging team players have an important role in pushing the team to take well-considered risks.

The real mark of effective Challengers is their knowing when to
stop pushing. If you are a real team player, you know when a
consensus has emerged and when it is time to move on. Team players will say, "I've had my day in court, all sides of the issues have
been discussed, and the team has reached a genuine agreement." A

team player supports the consensus and works toward its implementation unless a real legal or ethical concern remains.

The Challenger who does not know when to quit, when to acknowledge resolution of the issue, or when to move on can be an
obstructive force on the team. The perennial devil's advocate is not
a positive team player.

Challenger: A Summary

The Challenger is a team player who openly questions the goals,
methods, and even the ethics of the team, who is willing to disagree
with the team leader, and who encourages the team to take well-
considered risks.

Challenger: A Checklist of Behaviors

1. Candidly shares views about the work of the team
2. Is willing to disagree openly with the leadership of the team
3. Often raises questions about the team's goals
4. Pushes the team to set high ethical standards for work
5. Speaks out even when views are contrary to those of a vast
    majority of the team
6. Asks "why?" and "how?" and other relevant questions about
    presentations at team meetings
7. Sometimes is accused of not being a team player because he
    or she differs with the conventional wisdom
8. Challenges the team to take well-conceived risks
9. Is honest in reporting team progress and stating problems
    facing the team
10. Is willing to blow the whistle on illegal and unethical activ-
    ities of the team
11. Will back off when views are not accepted and will support
    a legitimate team consensus

Challenger: A Checklist of Adjectives

1. Candid
2. Ethical

3. Questioning
4. Honest
5. Truthful
6. Outspoken
7. Principled
8. Adventurous
9. Aboveboard
10. Brave

Team-Player Actions

Teams need many things to be successful, and a variety of team-player styles is one important dimension of effective teamwork. Conversely, a team player can contribute in many ways to the success of a team. There is no one clear description of a team player. A team player comes in a variety of uniforms with varied equipment.

The message for team players is "Affirm your style, your strengths, your specific contributions to the team effort. And do it well. Be the best Contributor, Collaborator, Communicator, or Challenger. In addition, recognize that you have the capacity to make greater use of the strengths of other styles. You can change. If you find that your effectiveness would increase by extending your team-player style, then plan and work toward the incorporation of additional strengths into your repertoire." In the end, the complete team player is able to use the strengths of all four styles as required by the situation. The situational determinants include the stage of team development (see Chapter Six) and the current team functions (see Chapter Eight).

The Team-Player Survey, found in Resource C, will give you a reading on your current primary team-player style. As you reflect on your behavior in teams, try to identify some situations that would be aided by actions associated with other styles. For example, my primary style is Communicator. A committee of which I am a member is overloaded with many other process people. The group clearly lacks someone who is willing to question important decisions. At a recent committee meeting, I extended my team-player style by objecting to a proposed decision and insisting that the group consider other alternatives. My opposition brought out similar opinions by other committee members who had been reluctant to speak out. While it was not easy to behave in an unfamiliar fashion, the result was satisfying. Clearly, it will be easier next time. It will also be easier for the other team members who saw the value of another style.

The message for corporate executives and high-level managers is "Expand your view of the team player to include all four dimensions—task, goal, process, and questioning. As you make decisions about team composition, team leadership, succession planning, and performance appraisal, consider this broader conception of the team player. And stop thinking of a team player as someone who simply 'fits in' and who will not 'rock the boat.' " In Chapter Eight, we describe methods of creating an organizational culture that supports positive team players.

Chapter Four

Ineffective Team Players

Sometimes we try too hard to help the team. We get so committed to the team effort, so absorbed in our view of what the team needs, that we become ineffective. We overemphasize the importance of task completion, goal direction, process, or challenging the status quo. Even though we have the best of intentions, we get to the point that Stuart Atkins called "too much of a good thing" (Atkins, 1981).

The team may be doing well and the team players may seem to be doing well when, almost without notice, one will go over the boundary. The effective team player becomes a drain on the team. The helpful comments are now barriers to success. In this case, there is such a thing as too much help—too much team play.

Some team members are particularly committed to one of our four styles. They believe that they have the key to a successful team. One negative result of this strong commitment is the inability to see clearly the usefulness of the other styles. These players may become impatient with team players who are trying to be helpful—but in other ways. Overly committed team players may exaggerate the dimensions of their own styles and push the team to do the same. Stresses such as time pressure, deadlines, and decreased revenues can lead to a lack of tolerance for other team players. Ironically, these are just the times when we need more effective team play.

The motivations for behavior are many and complex. Our purpose here is not to root out all causes of ineffective team players. However, observation tells us that some people try too hard to be helpful and, as a result, go beyond the zone of effectiveness. Their strength becomes a weakness. Observation also teaches us that the pressures of business lead to an impatience with alternative team-player styles. Style differences are seen as blocks to progress. On the other hand, some people have never learned how to be an effective team player. See Exhibit 1 for a list of questions to help you determine whether you are an ineffective team player.

The Cost of Ineffective Team Players

Ineffective team players cost the organization. Their behavior results in wasted time and effort, lost opportunities, poor customer relations, low morale, and high turnover. Ultimately, they have a negative impact on the bottom line. In mortgage banking, for example, loan originators who are ineffective Communicators fail to build positive relationships with the loan processors. The originators then spend more time on the loan packages and less time originating loans. The net result is decreased sales and usually turnover in the processor support group.

Mergers and acquisitions can be derailed by ineffective team players in key roles during the transition phase. If members of the transition team are not willing to collaborate on goals and plans, to pitch in and do what is necessary for the good of the new organization, and to be concerned about avoiding "throwing the acquisition's existing employees off balance" (Dionne, 1988, p. 16), the outcome could be disastrous in business and human terms.

Software development can be excessively time-consuming, costly, and frustrating without effective team players. Many software developers enjoy working alone and, therefore, have become ineffective team players. They are Contributors in the extreme. They issue high-quality technical work but sometimes fail to see where the systems fit into the business. And they may have poor interpersonal skills

Exhibit 1. Are You an Ineffective Team Player?

Responses: Yes (y), Sometimes (s), No (n)

_____ 1. When forming a new team, do you select only those people whose approaches are similar to yours?
_____ 2. When things are not going your way, do you sit quietly or sulk?
_____ 3. Are you impatient wiith other team members who want to discuss process issues?
_____ 4. Do you try to avoid or smooth over differences among team members?
_____ 5. Do you go along with some team decisions even though you are not sure going along is the right thing to do?
_____ 6. As a team leader, do you set goals without the real involvement of team members?
_____ 7. When things go wrong on the team, do you quickly blame the leader?
_____ 8. Do you bad-mouth the team to other people in the organization?
_____ 9. Do you miss deadlines for completion of team assignments or submit incomplete work?
_____ 10. Do you push for individual recognition of team members rather than team acknowledgment and awards?

Summary: If you answered "no" to all ten questions, skip to the next chapter.
If you answered "yes" or "sometimes" to at least five questions, stay tuned.
If you answered "yes" to all ten questions, start the book over again.

---

for dealing with users. Often, the outcome is a release that is late, does not meet user requirements, or requires extensive modification.

At a recent committee meeting, a conflict arose over the future direction of the team. The team leader negotiated an agreement with her boss and then announced the decision to the team. The team members disagreed with the decision and were upset about the process used to arrive at the decision. In an effort to smooth over the conflict, a compromise was proposed by one member and quickly supported by the team leader. However, it was a true compromise in the sense that it "split the differences" and satisfied no one. Ineffective team play led to a poor decision. Subsequently, two key people left the team.

The Ineffective Contributor

The task-oriented Contributor who helped the team by providing useful technical information, by always doing the required homework, and by being a model of excellence can become ineffective because of (1) data overload (reports that are too long and too detailed), (2) pushing for unrealistic performance standards, (3) losing sight of the big picture (the goal or charter of the team), or (4) a lack of patience with the need for a positive team climate. When things go wrong, the Contributor believes the solution is more and better information, reports, and presentations.

Ineffective Contributors abound in technical organizations. Their battle cry is "Let's be objective." For them, the goal of every business activity is to remove the human element. Therefore, the emphasis is on efficiency, following the rules, being correct, minimizing risk, reducing costs, and increasing the use of technology. As you might suspect, besides being ineffective, the Contributor can be pretty boring.

In a workshop on business ethics, an otherwise effective Contributor went over the line when he persisted in his position that all ethical decisions could be "objectified." He argued that all we needed were "facts" to determine what to do when faced with a dilemma. The problem, as he saw it, was that the case study simply did not provide the class with enough information. Other team members tried to explain that more facts were not going to change their opinions since they were strongly influenced by personal values and religious beliefs. His insistence on more and better data caused delays and bad feelings among team members.

The Ineffective Contributor: Adjectives

1. Data-bound
2. Shortsighted
3. Compulsive
4. Perfectionist
5. Uncreative

The Ineffective Collaborator

The goal-directed Collaborator pushes the team to develop a mission and goals and helps by pitching in, sharing resources, working outside his or her defined role, and doing what is required to maintain that commitment to the team goal or charter. But the Collaborator can become ineffective because of (1) failure to revisit or challenge periodically the mission or goals, (2) lack of attention to the basic team tasks and work-area performance, (3) failure to focus on meeting the needs of other team players ("The mission is everything!"), or (4) complaining publicly about team failures. When the team is perceived as decreasingly effective, the Collaborator believes the solution lies in greater commitment to the vision, mission, and goals of the team.

Ineffective Collaborators are typically found in middle management positions in organizations. They have read all the books on leadership and see themselves as an IIT (Iococca in Training). They work hard to be seen as forward-looking and visionary. In fact, they do a good job of creating a vision, developing a mission statement, and preparing goals. However, the process becomes an end in itself. They fail to realize that the process must be managed. Goals require objectives, action plans, and accountability. As status reports and other follow-up methods are needed to ensure process, the leader shifts to the role of manager. But the ineffective Collaborator has little patience for the work involved in managing the effort.

Ineffective Collaborators are insensitive to other team players who do not give as much attention to goals. Team players who insist that the team complete the day-to-day work tasks are seen as "grunts." Communicators who want to see an effective process for developing goals are not taken seriously. And Challengers who question the goals are viewed as obstructionists.

Ineffective Collaborators try to do too much. In an effort to be helpful to their colleagues, they jump in and take over from other team members. While the Collaborator sees the action as helpful ("I'm just rolling up my sleeves and pitching in"), other team players see it as unnecessary interference and control.

The Ineffective Collaborator: Adjectives

1. Overcommitted
2. Insensitive
3. Overinvolved
4. Too global
5. Overambitious

The Ineffective Communicator

The process-oriented Communicator who helped the team by effectively facilitating member involvement, conflict resolution, consensus building, and other positive climate management activities can become ineffective by (1) seeing team process as an end in itself ("Are we having fun yet?"), (2) failing to challenge or confront other team members, (3) not recognizing the equal importance of completing task assignments and making progress toward team goals, or (4) overuse of humor and other process techniques. When the team fails to make progress, the Communicator assumes the reason must be that "We don't work well together" and proceeds to push for increased emphasis on listening, feedback, and participation.

The ineffective Communicator usually can be found in the human resources department. He or she may have been to some seminars on group dynamics and may take it all in as gospel. For the Communicators, process becomes a new religion. They embrace it with all the fervor of an extremist. They see process problems everywhere, and they see the solution to all the organization's ills as better relationships among team members. As a result, they tend to alienate many people who might see the importance of positive process but who realize it is not the only dimension of effective teamwork. The worst thing that can happen to a Communicator who crosses the line and enters the ineffectiveness zone is not to be taken seriously by other team members. Other members wonder about someone who does not appear to be concerned about important business issues.

At the first meeting of a new business team, an ineffective Communicator with the best of intentions tried to begin by conducting several exercises designed to develop a positive climate. There was resistance from other team members, but she persisted in carrying out her plan. At the end of the meeting, it was explained to her that the timing was inappropriate. When a new team forms, people want to know something about team purpose, team roles, tentative timetable, and other fundamentals. After they feel comfortable with the task, they will be willing to deal with team process. In this case, the team was so upset it was not possible to discuss team norms and relationships for at least a month.

The Ineffective Communicator: Adjectives

1.   Aimless
2.   Foolish
3.   Placating
4.   Impractical
5.   Manipulative

The Ineffective Challenger

The Challenger who helps the team by candidly questioning the team's goals and methods, raising ethical issues, disagreeing with the leadership, and encouraging risk taking can become an ineffective team player by (1) not knowing when to back off and let the team move on, (2) pushing the team to take risks that are beyond reason, (3) becoming self-righteous, rigid, and inflexible, (4) painting himself or herself into a corner where challenging is an end in itself, or (5) using so-called honesty as a cover for attacks on other team members. When the team is not moving ahead, the Challenger believes that there is a lack of candor or innovativeness and that the solution lies in greater confrontation and risk taking.

The ineffective Challenger is found everywhere, but there seem to be more of them in manufacturing and in the blue-collar areas of government (for example, roads and public safety). These are people who love a fight. They enjoy walking the boundary line, getting a shot in at the boss, pushing the rules to the limit, or daring you to knock that chip off their shoulder. They enjoy the role of outsider, a sort of Clint Eastwood of the organization. Although the team needs people who will speak out with integrity about important issues, they do not need members who simply enjoy being disagreeable. Ineffective Challengers use the cloak of honesty to further their personal agendas. But in the final analysis, *their* actions are dishonest. Most important, they often divide the team and create unnecessary delays caused by the confrontations. In the end, the Challenger who goes over the boundary of effective behavior becomes, at best, an annoyance—a person to be tolerated.

One especially ineffective Challenger was a member of an advisory board of a nonprofit community agency. He said that he represented the underclass of the city and that the agency was not doing enough to help this group. While some of his objections to their programs were helpful, other board members did not consider them because (1) he seemed to oppose everything the agency did and (2) his manner was abrasive and included personal attacks on the staff. The more his points were ignored, the more confrontational and self-righteous he became. In the end, he became the "crazy radical," whom no one took seriously.

The Ineffective Challenger: Adjectives

1. Rigid
2. Arrogant
3. Self-righteous
4. Contentious
5. Nit-picking

Dealing with the Ineffective Team Player When It Is You

For individuals, awareness is the first step to behavioral change. It is important that we understand our team-player style and the potential that exists for ineffectiveness. Self-understanding and self-assessment can tell us our primary team-player style. Then we can use this information to become sensitive to the possibilities of overusing our strengths to the point of ineffectiveness. Contributors can pull back when they become too technical; Collaborators can stop when they overemphasize strategic issues; Communicators can put on the brakes when they get mired in group process; and Challengers can call a halt when opposition becomes an end in itself. Self-knowledge can help develop an appreciation of other team-player styles and, therefore, tolerance of different approaches to effective team play.

Self-understanding can be supplemented by the use of a self-assessment instrument. The Team-Player Survey (see Resource C) can give you a reading of your team-player style and potential weaknesses as a team player. The instrument is a form of self-feedback since it measures your perception of yourself. The results can lead to an acknowledgment of your strengths and a plan for improvement. The plan should include (1) ways to make better use of your strong points, (2) cutting back on the overuse of your style, (3) strategies for incorporating behaviors from some of the other styles, and (4) developing an appreciation of people who help the team in different ways.

Another alternative is to obtain feedback from other team members who have had an opportunity to observe you as a team player. You can ask for the feedback informally in a conversation, or you can use a structured feedback process facilitated by the use of a version of the Team-Player Survey completed by other team members. If that survey is not available, you can use the lists in this book.

Dealing with the Ineffective Team Player When It Is Someone Else

The following guidelines are especially directed at the team leader, but they are applicable to all team members who observe counter-productive team players.

Listen. Maybe, just maybe, the person has a point. Often what you perceive as ineffective team play is simply your inability to appreciate a person with another style. In these situations, his or her primary style may be your least active style, and vice versa. What you see as obstructionist may actually be effective challenging of a team decision. What you see as pie-in-the-sky thinking may actually be long-term goal setting. Listen—use your paraphrasing, questioning, and summarizing skills—before you play the lecturer.

Meet Privately. Ask the person questions such as these: "Why are you on this team?" "What do you see as your role?" "What concerns do you have about the way the team is going?" Probe to uncover the causes of resistance. It may be that he or she is experiencing a personal or family crisis and that this team responsibility comes at a bad time. It may be that the team member's style is in a distinct minority on the team, so he or she feels out of place. For example, a Communicator found herself on a team that had no interest in the process aspects of the team's operation. Unable to confront the team with her concerns, she sat silently through the meetings. The purpose of the private meeting is to uncover the needs of a person in this kind of situation and to determine if those needs can be satisfied on this team.

Reestablish Team Norms. Reestablishing team norms is recommended when there are several ineffective team players because it uses group process to deal with them. At the beginning or end of a meeting, someone (usually the leader) should facilitate a discussion of team member expectations, with the goal of developing a list of acceptable behaviors. You are looking for expectations in areas such as completing work assignments, attendance, starting and ending on time, participation in discussions, raising objections, format for presentations, decision making, and confronting differences. Team norms have two functions: (1) they provide a guide for self-monitoring by team members, and (2) they provide a basis for the team leader or member to give feedback to another member who has violated a norm. Often a discussion that centers on developing a set of team norms will lead to an assessment of the extent to which the norms currently are being followed.

Negotiate. Stated simply, negotiation involves an agreement in which I agree to do something if you agree to do something. For example, if you agree to back off your insistence that we clarify team-member roles until we get an agreement on our mission statement, I will let you lead a discussion on roles at the beginning of our next meeting. Negotiation often neutralizes a situation for the moment, but it may not eliminate the problem unless the negotiation leads to a permanent agreement on new behavior. For example, "I will allow a full consideration of the ethical aspects of product research if you agree to support fully all team decisions reached by consensus."

Positive Reinforcement. If the person does make a useful contribution, however small, try to make him or her feel good about that acceptable behavior. Reinforcement can send a message that this is the desired behavior. At a recent meeting, a team player who rarely spoke said, "What is the point of all this?" The leader responded, "That's a good question. How does this project fit into our overall team mission?" The team leader's response did two things: (1) it helped the individual team player, and (2) it helped the team focus on the need to see beyond the immediate tasks to the big picture.

Contact the Person's Boss. Sometimes your best efforts at listening, meeting, processing, negotiating, and reinforcing just do not work. You must go to the person's boss and discuss the problem. The boss may be able to give some insight into the team player's behavior, make a suggestion on how to handle the person, or offer to talk to the person directly. In one recent case, the boss acknowledged that this was an inappropriate assignment and agreed to remove the person from the team.

Confront the Person. Confrontation really means confronting the behavior exhibited by the person. This is best done privately. But sometimes privacy is not possible, and direct feedback during the meeting is necessary. You must be specific and point to the person's behavior that is inhibiting the team. You may elect to discuss how the behavior is affecting you. For example, "Stan, your insistence that we collect more data is slowing us down, causing us to miss deadlines and to renege on commitments to clients. Frankly, I'm frustrated because we have vigorously followed our action plan, and you are still not satisfied."

Zap the Person. Some people must go. Some people just cannot be rehabilitated. They must be transferred, reassigned, or simply fired.

Chapter Five

Team Players as
Team Leaders

It almost goes without saying, but let's say it anyway: the leader is critical to the success of a team. Our view of leadership has been changed dramatically in the past few years by Bennis (1988), Bennis and Nanus (1985), Block (1987), and Kouzes and Posner (1987). Leaders are people who create an inspired vision for the organization, communicate a sense of enthusiasm for the effort, and are honest and authentic in their interactions with people. But team leaders must also be effective managers. They need to see both the forest and the trees. Teams need to look ahead and to produce a quality product today. A team of programmers, for example, needs to consider the future possibilities of computing technology as well as to meet next month's deadline for the release of a new system. The human resources team needs to have a plan for the work force in the year 2000 while they get set to launch a series of seminars on business ethics next quarter.

The effective team leader is an effective team player. Effective team leadership requires the articulation of a vision, the creation of a clear mission, and the development of goals, objectives, and action plans. The most effective leaders involve team members in these activities. Effective team leaders ensure the completion of immediate tasks and work assignments in a high-quality and timely fashion. The most effective leaders inspire a desire to produce quality products and services and to provide excellent customer service. They have the ability to communicate with all team members and with important players outside the team. The most effective leaders have excellent skills in listening, conflict resolution, and consensus building. And they create an open environment in which members feel free to express their views with candor and integrity. The most effective leaders are challengers of the status quo and are supportive of others who push for risk taking and innovation.

A team player can be either a follower or a leader. Many people play both roles in an organization and, in fact, may play both roles during the same day. In the morning, you may attend the division staff meeting with the vice president as team leader. In the afternoon, you may hold a new product task force meeting where you serve as chairperson.

Your team-player style remains consistent as you make your transition from follower to leader and back again. However, the style may manifest itself in different ways depending upon the role.

As a member, the Contributor can be depended upon to provide accurate data in support of the team's effort, and as a leader, the Contributor structures the operations of the team to solve technical problems efficiently. In a leadership role, the Collaborator tends to be a strategic thinker, and as a follower, the Collaborator does what is required to keep the team moving toward its goals. Communicators as team leaders are noted for their participative management approach, and as members, they encourage and support the involvement of others through the use of their communication style. As a member, the Challenger raises questions about team issues and sometimes questions the leader; as the team leader, the Challenger models the devil's advocate in order to establish the norm of candor and openness.

In the final analysis, the style remains consistent as the roles change. As the roles change, the expectations of the person in the role vary. Leaders are expected to behave differently from followers, and they do. The behavior, however, is consistent with the team-player style. In the following sections, we will review five important leadership functions and how each style of team player carries them out.

The Contributor as Leader

The Contributor sees the team as a vehicle to solve business problems, with an emphasis on efficiency. The Contributor is guided by the philosophy "If it ain't broke, don't fix it." The most effective Contributor leaders are effective managers. They get things done and they get them done well.

Planning tends to be tactical in approach. The Contributor emphasizes short-term, specific, measurable objectives with detailed action plans. The planning process is data based with a heavy use of demographic statistics, reports of past results, and conservative forecasts.

Communication tends to be economical. The Contributor is a person of few words. Contributors do not waste time engaging in small talk (unless the culture requires it) because they like to get to the point and then get on with the work. In other words, Contributors do not see communication as work. They prefer written communication (especially memos) over oral communication. Presentations tend to be formal speeches with lots of overhead transparencies buttressed by detailed handouts. When it is perfected, the Contributor will probably latch onto a new class of software called "groupware." These programs are intended to improve communications and productivity among team members linked via a personal computer network. One package allows people on the network to annotate a document while another tracks tasks waiting to be done.

Risk taking tends to be conservative. The Contributor prefers well-researched, well-reasoned proposals. Change, in the view of the Contributor, is an incremental process backed up by a detailed plan. In a given period, risks should be limited in number. As a leader, the Contributor will push the team to make the existing system work better before trying new ventures.

Problem solving tends to be analytical. As a team leader, the Contributor provides the team with a structured model involving a step-by-step plan. Problem solving, as viewed by the Contributor, requires a careful assessment of data, use of technical expertise, and rigorous examination of costs and benefits.

Decision making tends to favor decisions that are practical, logical, and cost-effective. The Contributor ensures that the team's decisions are consistent with company policies and procedures and are in the mainstream of the corporate culture. As the team's leader, the Contributor expects decisions to be based upon clear evidence with the outcome well documented for the record.

The Contributor Leader: The Downside

As a leader, the Contributor can be too practical, too conservative, and overly task oriented. Contributors can be overcome with efficiency and forget about effectiveness. Teamwork becomes something to get through ("so we can get back to work") and not something to be enjoyed. Viewed from the outside, team meetings lack energy, enthusiasm, and warmth. It all looks rather dull and boring.

Leaders with narrow technical specialties seem to be most prone to becoming ineffective Contributor leaders. They covet the leadership position for the status and salary increase but dislike the interpersonal responsibilities that go with it and they often lack the vision to see beyond the immediate technical problem facing the team. As leaders of functional work teams, they often spend lots of time looking over the shoulders of team members and, in the extreme, step in and take over the problems.

The Contributor leader focuses the team on detailed problem solving but loses sight of member needs for inclusion, responsibility, and recognition. They also lose sight of the big picture—where the work of the team fits into team mission and goals.

The Collaborator as Leader

In a leadership role, the Collaborator might be described as a "shirt-sleeve visionary." The Collaborator sees the leader's role as providing a view of the future—focus, mission, goals. At the same time, he or she is ready to pitch in and help out as required. The Collaborator approaches the key leadership functions with a particular style:

Planning tends to be strategic. The planning process emphasizes long-term goals backed up by action plans that involve all team members. As a leader, the Collaborator will present these goals but will encourage member involvement and will be open to all views of the team's future. However, the team's goals must be consistent with the overall corporate plan.

Communication tends to focus on big-picture issues. The Collaborator lacks patience for detailed technical discussions. As a leader, he or she likes a lot of discussion on organizational direction and will regularly ask for input. The Collaborator is effective at managing the outside—communicating with other key players in the organization. The telephone is the preferred communication medium, although Collaborators are well-known for periodic memos on strategic direction.

Risk taking tends to focus on the potential gain of a given risk rather than the potential loss. As leaders, Collaborators are willing to take planned risks because they are confident they will be able to deal with unanticipated problems. While they believe "nothing ventured, nothing gained," they calculate all risks for their contribution to the team's mission and goals. Collaborators are known to take risks that stretch organizational policies and procedures in order to help the team achieve its goals. Their motto is "It is easier to get forgiveness than permission."

Problem solving tends to put all problems in some larger context. As a leader, the Collaborator looks for the implications of a problem and the impact of potential solutions on organizational effectiveness. Collaborators are often willing to pitch in and help out where necessary, to obtain the necessary resources for the team, and to ensure that the appropriate team members get credit for solving the problem.

Decision making tends to look at both sides of an issue and favor an open process. However, as a leader, the Collaborator wants all team decisions tied to the long-term strategy. Collaborators value commitment to all team decisions, and they work hard to ensure that everyone is willing to put his or her shoulder to the wheel. They will insist that the team revisit key decisions to assess results.

The Collaborator Leader: The Downside

As a leader, the Collaborator can become too global and overly ambitious, and can place too much emphasis on the long-term aspects of the team's mission. They want so badly to be visionary and forward-looking leaders that they lose sight of the work required to get to the future.

The Collaborator leader's enthusiasm for a strategic approach to team activities can be misplaced. I am familiar with a team leader who is too far out in front of the rest of the team. His push for strategic plans has not been well received by other team members because they feel the organization is currently poorly managed. Their view is that quality and customer service need to be significantly improved before any new ideas should be explored. The net result of this lack of consensus is tension, poor communication, and ineffective coordination.

The Collaborator leader who succeeds in putting shared visions and goals into place will often fail to manage the process. In one organization, a team spent two days in an off-site meeting developing a set of long-term goals. Six months later, they were still on flip-chart paper rolled up in a corner of the plant manager's office. This may be an extreme case (or is it?), because there is usually follow-up at least to the extent that the products of a planning meeting are printed and distributed to all team members. The ineffective Collaborator leader does not like to manage the real follow-up that involves monitoring progress, allocating resources, revising plans, and coordinating individual efforts.

The Communicator as Leader

In leadership roles, Communicators are highly participatory. They value a positive work climate, enjoy a family atmosphere, and believe a team that works well together is more effective. In carrying out the key leadership functions, Communicators pay particular attention to group process issues.

Planning tends to give heavy emphasis to the involvement of all team members in the development of the plan. For the Communicator, the process by which the plan is prepared is as important as the content of the plan. Communicators like to make sure that the plan is acceptable to everyone or at least that everyone has an opportunity to influence its direction.

Communication tends to be warm, relaxed, and generally enjoyable. As team leaders, Communicators make special efforts to have enjoyable team meetings. They realize that many people hate meetings and, therefore, will make sure the room is comfortable, have coffee served, chat with people prior to the meeting, use humor to break the ice, and use other climate-setting techniques. The Communicator is a good listener and is especially effective at informal one-on-one meetings with other members.

Risk taking tends toward risks that will improve the internal functioning of the team. The Communicator as team leader will want to explore fully the impact of a proposed action on the team climate and to ensure all members are aware of the possible consequences. A risk for the Communicator would be to give negative feedback to a member of the team.

Problem solving tends to favor quality circles and other high-involvement problem-solving approaches. As a team leader, the Communicator is able to communicate a sense of urgency and, if necessary, enthusiasm for a problem and the need to solve it. The Communicator believes strongly that people who are closest to the problem should be deeply involved in the development of the solution. The Communicator leader will try to facilitate an effective resolution of differences among members with varying opinions.

Decision making tends to be democratic. The Communicator in a leadership role likes to make sure all views have been heard before making a decision. On major decisions, he or she favors the consensus method. The Communicator will resist all efforts to buck decisions to the team leader or to a higher authority.

The Communicator Leader: The Downside

As a team leader, the Communicator can become obsessed with process and see interpersonal communication as the panacea for all team problems. He or she can emphasize climate setting to the point where team goals and the completion of work assignments are incidental to a "Let's party!" mandate. Even more destructive to the team is the development of norms that discourage internal criticism. The Communicator leader who is overly concerned with climate often discourages, smothers, or in other ways inhibits well-intentioned questioning of the team's work.

Leaders of teams in voluntary organizations and professional associations are especially prone to these excesses. Combine human resource–development or organization-development specialists together in a professional society, and you get strong potential for an obsessive concern for process.

Beware, too, of recent converts—leaders who receive feedback that they are too task oriented and, with a vengeance, try to become Communicators overnight. They take so much time and put so much effort into their process skills that they forget the team has a job to do.

The Challenger as Leader

As a team leader, the Challenger is no longer questioning authority (unless it is a higher authority) but is attempting to set a team norm of openness and candor. He or she wants all team members to have questions about the team's mission and methods and, in a leadership role, will continue to use a questioning mode in regard to reports, presentations, and overall team strategy. The Challenger has a unique approach to the key leadership functions.

Planning tends to push the team to consider new directions. The Challenger favors the use of brainstorming and other free-form planning techniques. He or she encourages the team to set aside self-limiting thinking ("It's not in the budget." "We tried that last year.") and to seek out new areas for change and growth. The Challenger does not worry if the plan goes against the grain; he or she pushes the team to set "stretch" objectives that go beyond the safe and predictable.

Communication tends to be open, direct, and, occasionally, confrontational. As a team leader, the Challenger does not beat around the bush. He or she uses questions to make points ("Do you think that . . . ?") and to bring out information ("Can you provide us with . . . ?"). Challengers like meetings as a communication vehicle because they enjoy the give-and-take of discussion and debate.

Risk taking tends to focus on the potential gain from every proposed team risk. As a leader, the Challenger is action oriented and likes to push the team to new frontiers. The Challenger has a high tolerance for uncertainty and failure but rarely talks about the possibility of failing. He or she encourages innovation and allows members the freedom to fail, because good tries are not punished. A Challenger is likely to say, "A mistake is just another way of doing something."

Problem solving tends to be unstructured. As a leader, the Challenger will push hard for identification of the real problem by peeling away the symptoms. He or she will raise tough questions about the problem analysis—especially about the data used to support the conclusions. The Challenger wants the team to develop many alternative solutions and, again, will insist that each alternative undergo careful scrutiny by the members.

Decision making tends to favor decisions that are "right," ethical, and, of course, legal. As the leader, the Challenger will weigh the facts and then encourage the team to use their experience to reach a conclusion. The Challenger talks a great deal about "gut" decisions and "judgment calls." He or she will also push to uncover hidden resistance on the part of team members and will encourage members to have all concerns addressed by the team before reaching a decision.

The Challenger Leader: The Downside

As leaders, Challengers can be too extreme in their positions, can waste resources on ill-conceived risks, and can offend others with their confrontational manner. They may push the team to develop projects that are presented as innovative but that lack good, basic data collection and analysis. Or they may promote projects that are well outside the mission of the organization. Ineffective Challenger leaders will often establish a tense climate in team meetings because they debate every issue and argue with team members. If a leader is a technical "guru," members will often be afraid to make presentations or offer opinions because of the fear of being "shot down" by the leader.

The team's image with external players can be adversely affected by a contentious Challenger leader. If the leader is the principal point of contact, he or she may offend key people in positions to help the team with budget, staff, and publicity. One extremely bright and creative team leader in a nonprofit agency was simply too confrontational in his interpersonal communication with key players from various funding sources. He saw them as dull and reactionary. They saw him as offensive. His ineffective style blocked people from seeing his many talents, and, in the end, the team lost many opportunities.

Personal-Development Planning for Team Leaders

A team leader will find it useful to identify his or her team-player style and to assess its effectiveness in the context of the needs of the team. The analysis of the impact of your style on the team can lead to a plan for improvement. The team may require a style of leadership that you are not providing. For example, a team in one of my client companies was extremely effective in delivering on its short-term commitments. The leader, an effective Contributor, was able to design and manage a production control system. She was also able to see the value of thinking strategically about future needs in technology and human resource development. In effect, she began to use some of the strengths of the Collaborator style. In another case, the leader of a user-developer problem-solving team was effective at getting the members to air their differences in a "civilized" fashion, but the net result was that people were being too polite. Following some feedback from me, she was able to move from the Communicator mode to use more of her Challenger strengths. The team needed more candor and openness, so she modeled and encouraged this behavior.

Successful Team-Building Strategies for Team Leaders

The most successful team leaders fuse the strengths of all four styles to create an effective team. Let's assume that you have been appointed leader of a start-up team or that you have assumed leadership of an existing team.

Get to Know the Team. Prior to any team activities, meet each team player informally. Share something of your background and experience as well as your feelings about this team. Try to find out each member's interests and possible concerns about the work of the team. If he or she has a particular motivation, see if that need can be met by participation on the team. The skills of the Communicator will be especially helpful here.

Define the Team's Purpose. Tell the team what you know about expectations, including timetable, budget, and constraints. Answer questions openly and look to address common concerns about the team's future. Engage the members in a discussion leading to a clear mission and goals. The goal-setting strengths of the Collaborator will be useful here.

Clarify Roles. Eliminate problems down the road by an early discussion of what is expected of each team player. On one cross-functional team, everyone was expected to brief his or her department about team progress; the leader was expected to deal with senior management; and others had responsibility for interfacing with specific players. The "grubby work" of taking minutes, setting up the meeting room, and preparing reports was rotated among team members.

Establish Norms. Early in the game, encourage the team to develop a list of norms or standards of behavior for team members. Whereas roles establish expectations, norms provide members with guidelines on how to work together. Here is a list generated at the first meeting of a task force expected to have a six-month life:

- We honor our commitments.
- We are willing to disagree.
- We are willing to allow disagreement.
- We attend all meetings.
- We start meetings on time.
- We pitch in and help out each other.
- We maintain confidentiality.

Draw Up a Game Plan. Mission and goals begin the planning process. Effective leaders insist that the team prepare objectives and action plans to ensure success in achieving the mission and realizing the goals. The plan also lets everyone know his or her assignments and due dates. The plan is a management tool for the leader to use in assessing progress, allocating resources, and preparing reports. The task strengths of the Contributor will be useful here.

Encourage Questions. The norm of "We are willing to allow disagreement" should be mandatory for all teams. The team leader is critical to the establishment of a climate that supports the expression of differences. Demonstrate your willingness to question the status quo, and be open to comments that overtly disagree with your position. The most powerful motivator of team-member behavior is the modeling of that behavior by the team leader; almost as powerful are support and encouragement from the leader. The Challenger's strengths are appropriate here.

Share the Limelight. Give recognition to individual team-player contributions and acknowledge team results. When opportunities for external recognition arise, spread the light around. Whether it is a presentation to senior management, an article in a company publication, or a picture in the local newspaper, give everyone a chance for recognition.

Be Participatory. Involve as many team members as possible in the work of the team. Spread around the work assignments as much as you can—especially the ones that mean positive exposure (making a presentation) and ones that are basically "no-brainers" (collating the handouts). When important decisions arise or key problems must be solved, use the consensus method. A consensus decision requires involvement and usually results in a better outcome.

Celebrate Accomplishments. The best teams work hard and play hard. As a team leader, you should encourage the team to plan celebrations to mark milestones, product launches, meeting of quotas, and other significant events.

Assess Team Effectiveness. Teams, like individuals, periodically need to take stock of themselves. As a leader, you should be the person to initiate this process. If you have just assumed leadership, this would be a good time to engage the team in a systematic review. And then, at least once a year, the team should ask and answer some basic questions:

- What are our strengths?
- Is our mission still valid?
- Are we making progress toward our goals?

Table 7. The Team Player as Leader.

Style/Function	Contributor	Collaborator	Communicator	Challenger
Planning	• tactical • statistical • specific • measurable • conservative	• strategic • visionary • open • big picture • involving	• total involvement • wide acceptance • agreement on process	• likes new directions • pushes for "stretch" objectives • questions value • more strategic than tactical • favors brainstorming
Communication	• economical • written • formal • to the point • detailed	• general • verbal • uses telephone • unstructured • organizational	• warm and friendly • informal • uses humor • emphasizes comfort • listens	• open • candid • confrontational • questioning • prefers meetings
Risk Taking	• conservative • incremental • planner • pilot tested • researched	• liberal • open to all ideas • goal directed • accepts risks • planner	• explores impact on team process • favors process risks • discusses consequences of risks • gives feedback	• focuses on potentials • pushes the frontiers • encourages innovation • supports "good tries"
Problem Solving	• analytical • structured • data based • technical • rigorous	• looks for context • looks for implications • pitches in • gives credit • gets resources	• favors involvement • uses quality circles • emphasizes process • facilitates conflicts • favors hands-on solutions	• unstructured • looks for "real" problem • questions analysis • examines data • costs versus benefits
Decision Making	• logical • mainstream • cost-effective • practical • consistent	• open to both sides • consistent with goals • looks for commitment • revisits decisions • wants involvement	• participative • uses consensus • resists leader control	• legal • ethical • "right" • probes for resistance

- How effective are team meetings?
- How well do we work with other parts of the organization?
- Is there clarity about team member roles?
- Are we satisfied with the quality of our work?
- How do our customers feel about us?
- What changes do we need to make?
- Is it still fun?

The Team-Development Survey in Resource A may produce other ideas for a team assessment.

Chapter Six

Adaptive Team Players

Much like individuals, teams experience stages of development. Teams mature from early formation through various phases to a developed organization—provided certain positive actions are taken. Teams, again like individuals, can get stuck in an immature phase and can suffer a case of arrested growth and ineffectiveness. Team players have an important role to play in each stage. Effective team players can successfully move a team toward maturity with specific, positive actions.

Tuckman (1965) identified four stages of team development:

1. Forming
2. Storming
3. Norming
4. Performing

In the *forming* stage, team members test the waters to determine what type of behavior will be acceptable, what the nature of the team's task is, and how the group will be used to get the work done. Forming is a period of dependency during which members look to the leader, to other team members, or to some existing rules for guidance. Tuckman compared this stage to that period of orientation and dependency experienced by infants and very young children.

The second stage, characterized by conflict among team members and resistance to the task, is *storming*. Storming is characterized by hostility among team members and toward the leader as members resist the structure of the group. Similarly, there is some resistance to the team's task—although the nature of the resistance will vary with the type of task. For example, an impersonal technical task will not evoke as much emotionality as will a team-building exercise. Often the leader's style will prevent the conflict of the storming stage from surfacing in a natural fashion. As a result, the resistance will emerge in unproductive ways (for example, not living up to commitments). Tuckman compared the storming of a team to the rebelliousness of a young child toward parental and school controls.

A sense of group cohesion develops in the third stage. This *norming* stage is characterized by acceptance of the team, a willingness to make it work, and the development of team norms. Norms are standards of behavior that the team develops for guiding member interaction and for dealing with the task. Information is freely shared and acted on, and openness and trust emerge among team members. This team development stage is comparable to the socialization phase associated with child development.

As interpersonal relationships become stabilized and as roles are clarified, the team moves into the fourth and final stage, *performing*. The group has a structure, purpose, and role and is ready to tackle the task. The emphasis here is on results, so positive problem solving and decision making take place. With interpersonal problems in the past and a focus on the real problems of life, this stage is compared to the mature phase in human development.

Tuckman's four stages of team development are a model—a convenient way of analyzing a team and the role of team players during each stage. The model is a tool—not a consistent picture of the real world. The real history of organizational teams can be a bit messier. Some teams begin by storming and then revert to the goal setting usually associated with the forming phase. At the same meeting, some members will act as if there were an agreement on norms while a few are still shouting each other down.

Team players should look for the dominant theme of the team—a theme that reflects the stage of development. Once you identify the stage, a quick assessment should reveal the team's needs and your role in helping the team successfully negotiate its way to maturity.

Forming

This first stage focuses primarily on the start-up of a new team. The same dynamics may occur when a new leader takes over a team or when there is a significant change in team composition or when the team's charter is altered. In effect, there is a re-formation.

During the forming stage, there is a lack of clarity about the purpose of the group and about the expectations of the members. Members do not know each other, so they tend to be polite and obedient. Typically, they want to be told what to do, member status is based upon their outside roles, and interactions and discussions are superficial and tend to be directed to the formal leader.

Contributor. At this stage, the Contributor wants to know what his or her role will be on the team. At the same time, there is a strong concern about expectations: What will I be expected to do? How much time will this take? Am I up to it? What specific tasks will I be responsible for?

As a Contributor, here is how you can help:

1. Initiate a discussion of possible team tasks.
2. Suggest that team members contribute information or opinions on the issue, based upon their area of expertise.
3. Offer to study an aspect of the problem and report at the next meeting; suggest that other team members do the same.
4. Ask the leader to provide directions to the team on team procedures (for example, frequency of meetings, length, location, minutes, agenda). If you are the leader, make sure this is on the agenda for the first meeting.

Collaborator. The Collaborator wants to know the mission or goal of the team. While Collaborators may have some ideas about the team's direction, they usually wait for the leader to define the purpose.

If you are a Collaborator, you can help:

1. Ask the leader to provide his or her view of the team's purpose. If you are the leader, structure a discussion designed to create a team mission. Share your views with the team.
2. Offer your opinion on the mission of the team.
3. Encourage other team members to provide their views of the mission.
4. Suggest that the team develop goals that support the mission.

Communicator. As the team is forming, Communicators want to know "who has been invited to the party." They have a need to make personal contact with other team members. Concerns include these: Who are these people? Will they accept me? What resources do they bring to the team?

During the forming stage, the Communicator can do several things to help:

1. Introduce yourself to as many people as possible prior to the meeting.
2. Ask the leader to explain how the team membership was selected. If you are the leader, speak with each person prior to the first meeting or discuss it at the first meeting.
3. Suggest that all members introduce themselves early in the first meeting.
4. Suggest that the team create a "talent bank" listing each person's areas of expertise.

Challenger. Challengers begin with a skeptical view of the team. They see it as "another do-nothing committee" or "more meetings that take me away from my real job." The Challenger wants to be sure the team will accomplish something useful and that the group will deal openly and honestly with issues.

As a Challenger, you can be useful to the team:

1. Ask the group if they are satisfied with the team's mission.
2. Openly express your reservations about the team's purpose or methods.
3. Raise questions for the leader. If you are the leader, encourage members to ask questions and maintain a non-judgmental at-

titude. If possible, meet with each person privately and try to answer his or her questions.

4. Suggest an exercise that asks each team member to express concerns about the team's charter, goals, methods, membership, and individual member roles.

Storming

The initial reluctance to express opinions is followed by a period of disagreement. Members feel free to disagree with each other and with the leader. Some of the questions, concerns, and even frustrations that people brought with them are now expressed. Ideas are challenged, closely evaluated, and sometimes "shot down." Members form alliances resulting in subgroup conflict, questions arise about both the task and process of the team, and there is some task avoidance as members enjoy the arguments.

Some teams never go through this stage because they are fearful that the expression of differences will tear the team apart. However, the conflict need not be heated or counterproductive. Quite the contrary; teams that fail to experience storming never learn how to deal with differences. As a result, they develop a form of passive resistance whereby members simply go along with the leader or a small cadre of members even though they are not really in agreement. Teams that have not successfully passed through the storming phase tend to be more divided and less creative.

Contributor. Contributors are concerned that this stage will result in a failure to get the basic job done. They wonder whether all this heat will ultimately shed any real light on the subject. The Contributor is concerned about the need to conduct an objective, factual examination of the team problem rather than just presenting opposing opinions.

During the storming stage, the Contributor should do the following:

1. Remain objective and encourage other team members to look at both sides of all issues.
2. Ask people for data to support their opinions.

3.   Remind the team of the need to complete their homework.
4.   Suggest that the team go forward with its basic task assign-
     ments.

Collaborator. During storming, the Collaborator is concerned
about the team's need to see the big picture. He or she wonders
whether these conflicts will detract from team efforts to move forward, in a coordinated fashion, toward the goals. The Collaborator
does not want to see team differences result in failure to pitch in and
help out each other. In the final analysis, the Collaborator worries
that team conflicts will dilute member commitment to the overall
team purpose.

The team can benefit from the Collaborator:

1.   Be open to ideas and encourage others to do the same.
2.   Ask how opinions expressed affect the team's mission and
     goals.
3.   Be prepared to revise mission and goals based upon opinions
     and data.
4.   Be willing to help out other team members.

Communicator. Among the four styles, the Communicator feels
most comfortable and potentially has the most to contribute during
the storming stage. Communicators understand that conflict among
members is useful as long as it is expressed in a positive manner.
They want to be sure that the team establishes effective norms regarding the expression of opinions and the resolution of differences,
and they are concerned that members listen to each other, discuss
the merits of the issue, and not engage in personal attacks.

At this stage, the Communicator can help the team in several
ways:

1.   Model good listening skills (for example, paraphrasing), and
     encourage others to do the same.
2.   Suggest norms for resolving differences (for example, con-
     sensus).
3.   Involve quiet members in discussion.
4.   Encourage the leader to ensure all sides are heard and, if no

agreement is possible, to make a decision. If you are the leader, enforce norms regarding positive communication and conflict resolution.

Challenger. Challengers are likely to be key players during the storming stage. They will test the team and the leader on issues of task and process, and they want to know whether the team will be receptive to tough questions that go to the core of the team's mission and goals. At this point, the Challenger will push the team to explore the limits of their mandate and to consider the innovative aspects of their problem.

The Challenger can be useful to the team:

1. Model positive confrontational behavior (for example, challenge the issue, not the person).
2. Be willing to back off when a clear consensus emerges.
3. Acknowledge the team leader and other members when they listen to your ideas.
4. Push the team to take well-conceived risks and innovative approaches to their problems.

Norming

As teams emerge from the storming phase, they learn from their successful experience in dealing with each other. The team establishes guidelines for resolving conflict, making decisions, interpersonal communication, completing assignments, and the management of meetings. Shared leadership becomes apparent. The development of these norms also leads to an increase in trust. It becomes possible to disagree with each other without the conflict leading to a personal attack. Members begin to enjoy the meetings and each other. A competitive cohesion develops as the team feels superior to other teams, and there is the laughing and joking that is associated with the informality of effective teams. But behind the surface of all these positive elements lurks the potential for groupthink; the competitive and informal climate can inhibit members from willingly challenging the prevailing thinking.

Contributor. The Contributor has an important role to play at this stage as task accomplishment goes forward. With positive norms established, the team is positioned to get on with the work. However, with the potential for groupthink, the Contributor is concerned that standards may be compromised and lower quality accepted.

To assist the team during the norming state, the Contributor should do the following:

1. Insist on high quality standards for all team output.
2. Help the team make effective use of its technical resources.
3. Push the team to prioritize its key tasks and to allocate assignments among members.
4. Take responsibility for getting important tasks done, and do not wait to be told what to do.

Collaborator. At the norming stage, Collaborators wonder whether this era of good feeling is detracting from a focus on the team mission and goals. They agree that positive norms are important and that good feelings and mutual support are necessary. But the real question is "Are we making progress toward our targets?" The Collaborator sees the establishment of norms as the basis for team members working together for team goals and being willing to share the limelight with each other.

As a Collaborator, you can help the team:

1. Keep the team focused on the big picture.
2. Encourage the team to revisit the mission and goals to determine if the commitment still exists.
3. Be open to altering the mission and revising the goals.
4. Insist that recognition for team efforts be given to all members.

Communicator. At this stage, the Communicator feels that all the struggle to establish a positive team climate has finally paid off. Shared leadership has emerged, trust is increasing, and conflicts are being resolved. However, there is a concern about too much of a good thing. The Communicator wonders whether the drive for consensus is masking some real disagreements. He or she senses that members are "walking on eggshells" because they are afraid to damage the effective group process. If you are a Communicator, you can be useful:

1. Remind the team that disagreements are acceptable and that, in fact, resolving differences is the hallmark of an effective team.
2. Suggest that the team conduct an internal assessment of their team process.
3. Use your feedback skills to point out behaviors that contribute to groupthink.
4. Remind the team that consensus decision making does not require that members simply go along with other members' views.

Challenger. With groupthink a distinct possibility, the Challenger is alert to the negative norm of reluctance to express differences. As members feel positive about their team and competitive with other teams, the Challenger worries that the tough questions will not be asked. He or she believes that the members can confront each other while still presenting a unified front to the outside world.

As a Challenger, you can help the team at this stage:

1. Ask tough questions, and encourage other members to do the same.
2. Where appropriate, challenge the leader. (This may help establish the norm that challenging is acceptable behavior.) If you are the leader, be open to minority views.
3. Confront the groupthink issue by asking, "Are we smoothing over basic disagreements?"
4. Encourage risk taking in team decisions and planning.

Performing

This is the payoff stage. The team is sailing along; they have learned how to be a team; there is agreement on goals, roles, and norms, and members are aligned toward producing results. The suppression of the storming stage has been worked through, and there is creative confrontation and innovative problem solving.

Moreover, the team is willing periodically to assess its performance and to take corrective action, and members take initiative and responsibility without waiting for direction from the leader. The team has achieved significant milestones. Their progress toward goals is noticeable, so team celebrations take place and recognition comes from other parts of the organization. Ongoing team concerns, however, can include complacency, failure to keep current, and a tendency to slip back into the bad habits of earlier stages. Members often enjoy the road to success, but, once they achieve it, look for other worlds to conquer.

Contributor. As the team achieves success, the Contributor sees a tendency to let due dates slip, failure to complete assignments, and lower attendance at meetings (or the sending of substitutes). He or she also worries that the team will not react quickly or effectively to changes in the external environment. The Contributor wants to be sure the team's skills and resources are sufficient to meet the new challenges.

If you are a Contributor, try to do the following:

1. Push the team to maintain high standards and live up to new task commitments.
2. Suggest that the team examine its resources and consider changing its membership to meet current needs.
3. Suggest that training or other development activities may be needed.
4. Recommend new and challenging task assignments.

Collaborator. Collaborators see the performing stage as a chance to look for opportunities to expand the mission or extend the goals. They correctly see stagnation as a real possibility for the team and, therefore, believe "visioning" new futures may be the answer.

At this stage, the Collaborator can be helpful:

1. Facilitate brainstorming sessions geared to the creation of a new future for the team.
2. Challenge the team to set aside past restrictions in creating revisions.

3. Ensure that all of the key players participate in this visioning activity.
4. Recommend the development of a new milestone chart.

Communicator. Communicators view the performing stage as the time to celebrate accomplishments. They will play an important role in recommending ways the team can reward itself and facilitating the involvement of the team members in planning the events. The Communicator, however, is concerned that stagnation indicators (poor attendance, assignments not completed) may lead to "process backsliding" and members becoming annoyed with each other. For example, a member is mad because her counterpart on the team has been sending a junior person to the meeting in her place. She, in turn, attacks their department at a subsequent meeting. Interpersonal relationships begin to resemble the storming stage.

Useful actions by the Communicator include the following:

1. Encourage positive, uplifting celebrations that involve all team members.
2. Challenge the team to maintain their norms or to develop new norms.
3. Give positive feedback to members who live up to their commitments.
4. Outside of team meetings, speak to members who show signs of backsliding.

Challenger. Challengers are key players at the performing stage because they can address the possible complacency. While the team success is a source of satisfaction, Challengers worry that the era of good feeling, with its parties and awards, may mask a fear of speaking up. They are also concerned that the team may not react boldly to internal changes (new leader, new members, new tasks) or to external changes (decreased revenues, increased competition, new laws) that impact the team.

As a Challenger, you can help:

1. Confront the team with indicators of stagnation.
2. Question assumptions of success.

Table 8. How Team Players Adapt to Team Development.

Stage/Style	Contributor	Collaborator	Communicator	Challenger
CONCERNS (F O R)	• My role • Expectations of me • Time commitments • My tasks	• Mission of team • Goals • Leader's vision of team	• Membership • Acceptance • Inclusion • Resources of members	• Is the team serious? • Openness • Receptivity to leader
POSITIVE ACTIONS (M I N G)	• Initiate discussion of tasks and roles. • Ask leader for direction. • Offer to take on a start-up assignment.	• Ask for leader's views. • Offer your view. • Suggest a discussion of team mission and goals.	• Ask how members were selected. • Ask that members introduce themselves. • Suggest a team "talent bank."	• Ask if team is satisfied with mission. • Express your reservations. • Suggest a discussion of member concerns.
CONCERNS (S T O R)	• More heat than light? • Will any work get done? • Can we be objective?	• Can we move forward? • Will conflicts lead to failure to help others? • Will conflicts dilute commitment?	• Will members listen? • Will members attack each other? • Will members look at both sides?	• Will team be receptive to minority opinions? • Will leader allow differences to surface? • Will team be open to revising its mission?
POSITIVE ACTIONS (M I N G)	• Ask for data to support opinions. • Remind team of need for homework. • Remain objective.	• Be willing to help others. • Ask how opinions impact team mission. • Be open to new ideas.	• Model good listening. • Suggest norms for resolving conflicts. • Encourage the expression of all views.	• Model positive confrontational behavior. • Be willing to back off when a consensus emerges. • Push the team to take well-conceived risks.

N O R M I N G	**CONCERNS**	• Will standards be maintained? • Will all resources be used?	• Will the team stay focused on goals? • Will we continue to make progress?	• Is drive for consensus masking real disagreements? • Will emphasis on process go too far?	• Will tough questions continue to be asked? • Will risk taking be reduced?
	POSITIVE ACTIONS	• Insist on high-quality work. • Push for priority setting. • Take responsibility; don't wait to be asked.	• Keep the team focused on the big picture. • Ask the team to revisit goals periodically.	• Remind the team that consensus does not eliminate disagreement. • Suggest an assessment of team process. • Use feedback skills.	• Ask tough questions and encourage others to do so. • Confront groupthink. • Encourage risk taking.
P E R F O R M I N G	**CONCERNS**	• Will team slip on responsibilities? • Will team react quickly? • Will members stay current on issues?	• Is it time for a new mission? • Does the team need to revise goals?	• Will team take the time to acknowledge success? • Will members revert to lack of concern for process?	• Will team react badly to changes? • Will members confront signs of stagnation?
	POSITIVE ACTIONS	• Push to maintain standards. • Propose an examination of needs and resources. • Recommend new and challenging assignments.	• Facilitate brainstorming sessions focusing on the future.	• Initiate positive celebrations of accomplishments. • Challenge the team to maintain norms. • Give feedback to members.	• Confront team with indicators of stagnation. • Initiate discussion of environmental changes. • Question assumptions of success.

3. Recommend that the team assess its current resources against the work that remains to be done.
4. Initiate a discussion of internal and external changes, their impact on the team, and the implications.

How Team Players Adapt to Team Development

Table 8 presents a convenient summary of the relationships between styles and stages. It suggests that each stage of team development evokes different concerns and questions depending upon style. Equally important are the series of recommended actions for each style at each stage. The effective team player provides the team with the assistance needed in an effort to move the team successfully through the stages toward the goal of performing.

In the next chapter, we combine the concepts of styles and stages in a strategy for analyzing and improving your team.

Chapter Seven

Analyzing Your Team's Strengths and Weaknesses

The most effective teams have a balance of team-player styles. They are equally concerned with (1) completing their work in a high-quality manner, (2) reaching their goals with a strong commitment, (3) developing and maintaining a positive team climate, and (4) raising questions about the team's goals and methods.

The effective teams know that having balance does not mean equal use of all styles at all times. Balance means having the capability to use the various styles when required by the team. A team's need for a particular style is situational and, as we suggested in Chapter Six, often based upon the stage of team development.

Stages and Styles: The Right Mix at the Right Time

The Collaborator can be especially helpful during the forming stage of a team when members are concerned about the team's purpose. Members come to the first meeting of a team with questions such as "Why was this team formed?" and "Where are we going?" Teams in the forming stage need someone who can provide structure for a discussion that will culminate in a statement of purpose (charter, mission) and direction (vision, goals, objectives).

When conflicts arise in the storming stage, the Communicator can facilitate a resolution of the differences. Team members need to understand that it is OK to express divergent opinions. The most creative teams learn how to resolve conflict in a positive manner—

127

by open discussion of the advantages and disadvantages. Teams in this stage need someone who can both encourage the expression of differences and help the team establish norms for civilized disagreement.

During the norming stage, the Contributor can help the team establish norms that foster high-quality performance and norms that ensure members assume responsibility for task accomplishment. Following the storming phase, meetings are fun and competitive cohesion develops as the team feels superior to other teams. At this point, the team needs to focus on getting the job done while they maintain the positive climate.

The performing stage is the goal of team development, and, therefore, one would assume no help to be necessary. At this stage, the team has learned how to be a team, norms are in place, and there is agreement on goals, roles, and tasks. Conflicts are successfully resolved, and the team is making great progress. This is the time for a celebration of accomplishments but it is also a time to be alert to the possibility of stagnation and regression. At this stage, we often begin to see signs of declining interest in the form of missed deadlines, sending substitutes (usually junior people) to meetings, and loss of the creative spark. The team needs someone to challenge their complacency, to question assumptions, and to suggest that the old fire, associated with the quest for success, has been lost.

The Goal: Style Diversity

Teams that include all four styles will typically outperform those teams that do not. Covering all four areas means that the team is not subject to the vulnerabilities that can be present when one or two styles are absent during an important period.

It would not be surprising to find teams with excessive strength in one or two styles to the exclusion of others. Most people hire and recruit team members for their similarity of strengths. Those hiring prefer working with people who have a similar style. Many team leaders do not look to broaden the team's perspective by bringing in people who have different styles. In this way, these leaders unknowingly contribute to the ineffectiveness of the team. Although team leaders usually seek team diversity by recruiting people from a wide variety of disciplines or work experiences, a diversity of technical expertise may not accomplish the goal of diversity of team-player styles.

Style Overload

When a team has many people with the same primary style and excludes other styles, the result is an excess of team strength in one area. Style overload can mean the team excels in several areas but may be weak in others. Depending upon the stage of team development, this lack of balance can have a significant impact on team effectiveness.

Contributor Overload. When a team has an excess of people whose primary style is Contributor, a great deal of work gets done and most of that work will be very high quality. The group is likely to make efficient use of its time and resources. Meetings are short, discussions are brief, and reports are limited but relevant. In lieu of meetings, memos are circulated to team members for comment. When possible, electronic mail, teleconferencing, conference calls, and other high-tech communication methods are used in place of face-to-face interaction. There is a free sharing of ideas, information, and skills, and members see each other as colleagues linked by technical expertise in the vein of an academic community.

The downside of Contributor overload is that members become intrigued by the intricacies of technical problems and tend to lose sight of the big picture. They enjoy the problem solving so much that they forget to ask why. The team may lose sight of its goal and how the immediate task, issue, or problem relates to the long-term purpose of the team. Fear of alienating a colleague may block people from asking tough questions about the team's work or from raising ethical issues. And team get-togethers may be so efficient that they lack the spontaneity and fun associated with effective teams.

Collaborator Overload. Upper-level teams in organizations tend to be more strategic in their orientation—with a potential for an excess of people with Collaborator as their primary style. This team feels comfortable with visioning exercises and enjoys blue-sky thinking. An annual strategic planning retreat would be a standard event for this team. They produce elaborate plans with detailed charts, and members of the team use references to the future in their presentations and conversations. All current projects are linked to some aspect of the plan. Team members find clever ways to work around the system to obtain resources or to bend the rules if required by the team; the company newspaper carries pictures and stories about team accomplishments; and members of the team are always asking each other questions such as "What do you need?" and "How can I help?"

While a major concentration on the future is positive, it is sometimes associated with a low concern for the present (for example, short-term objectives, immediate problems, and corporate requirements). Big-picture people often lack a healthy respect for the solution of technical problems or reports required by the organization. Moreover, Collaborator overload can also mean a low concern for the individual needs of members because so-called strategic team players sometimes forget that members need to participate in the discussions, to obtain recognition for their work, to get feedback, and, in a variety of other ways, to have the team acknowledge them as people. The strong push for commitment by this type of team can also result in a reluctance to criticize anything.

Communicator Overload. Team meetings with an excess of Communicators are usually relaxed and enjoyable. In fact, this asset of the team is often emphasized, as in a recent meeting notice that assured me, "We will definitely have fun." Members are very concerned with how other members feel about issues being discussed. Phrases such as "Are you comfortable with this?" and "Can you live with it?" are common. High-level listening skills are exhibited as members paraphrase, respond nonverbally, and allow others to finish their thoughts. There are regular process checks as someone will ask, "How are we doing?" Communicator overload is usually associated with "flip chart mania," as the meeting room walls are covered with chart paper. Most decisions are made by consensus and shared leadership is the norm.

The downside of fun meetings is that task accomplishment may not be sufficient to satisfy the oustide world. Some team members may even wonder whether there should not be more output for the time spent by the team. They may even wonder if there is not a better way to have fun! The context may be missing; the process is good but to what end? These teams may forget that a positive climate is means to an end and not the goal of a team.

Challenger Overload. When a team has an excess of people with Challenger as their primary style, rank does not have any privileges. Members are outspoken and even critical of the team leader. There are no controversies swept under the rug and no hidden agendas. Candor and openness are the norm. These teams tend to be very creative, even innovative in a variety of ways, and they support and encourage risk taking; failures are not punished. Assessments of team progress are honest and carefully scrutinized by team members. Team meetings are marked by pointed questions about goals, plans, and process.

Challenger overload can result in candor for the sake of candor. The team can get bogged down in always focusing on what is wrong. Members look for problems rather than strengths or opportunities (the glass is always half empty rather than half full). The outside world comes to see them as a group of whiners or weirdos.

Missing Perspectives

Another tool for analyzing your team is to look for the missing perspective—the one style that does not exist with any degree of strength. The absence of the strengths incorporated in that style will result in an imbalance leading to decreased effectiveness, missed opportunities, poor use of team resources, and even dissatisfaction among team members. The missing perspective is especially significant during the stage of team development when that style is most needed.

Contributor Is Missing. The main problem likely to emerge on a team with no Contributor is the lack of task focus. The team will not be serious about getting the necessary work done in an efficient manner; there will be a poor use of time and resources; meetings

will not be well planned and organized; and ultimately, there will
be a ripple effect—the few people who do complete their assignments will become resentful of those who do not, and eventually
even the effective few will lower their standards. And during the
start-up of a new team or the re-forming of an existing team,
members will fail to establish clarity on role definition and
expectations.

Collaborator Is Missing. Especially at the outset of the formation
of a team with no Collaborator, there will be a lack of clarity about
perspective and purpose. When the Collaborator style is missing, a
new team is likely to flounder and lose interest because goals are not
formulated. In general, the team is characterized by nonexistent or
unclear mission and goals. Members have a go-it-alone mentality;
there is no crossover assistance from people in other functional
areas. Lack of the collaborative perspective also means that only the
team leader or a few of the members get the recognition for team
accomplishments. In the end, other team members become resentful
because of the uneven distribution of credit for the team's success.

Communicator Is Missing. If there is no Communicator, the team
climate is formal, even tense, with a corresponding low level of
interpersonal comfort. Interactions among members are task and
goal based, with little concern for process issues. There is plenty of
talking and presenting of ideas but not much listening or responding to each other. Few decisions are made by the consensus method;
most issues are decided by a small minority or by majority vote.
Genuine participation by members is neither emphasized nor encouraged by the leader or members, and, as a result, involvement is
limited. Team success is measured by task completion. There is
little positive recognition or praise for individual contribution or
team accomplishments, and the prevailing philosophy is "It's your
job and that's what we pay you for."

Challenger Is Missing. With no one around to challenge the con-
ventional wisdom, the tendency for groupthink (Janus, 1972) is
great because the team culture includes strong pressures to conform.
Similarly, "The Abilene Paradox" described by Jerry Harvey (1974,

p. 23) in his classic article holds that teams often do things "in contradiction to the data they have for dealing with problems and, as a result compound their problems." Team members do not express their reservations because they believe they are the only ones who feel that way. It is paradoxical because there is no conformity pressure. The need for the Challenger's strengths is especially apparent in the performing stage, when the team has achieved some success and the members are feeling good about their progress. The team may wink at ethical constraints or legal obstacles in the surge to complete their work and obtain recognition, but there is also a tendency to play it safe in an effort to ensure their success. Risk taking will not be encouraged and surely not rewarded, so the potential for stagnation is great. Unless challenged to reexamine their goals and methods, the team may retreat, members will lose interest, and some may drop out.

How to Analyze Your Team

The team leader, in concert with the members, may analyze the team using the concept of team-player styles. The team looks for the potential of style overload and the possibility of a missing style, and once the situation has been identified, the team can assess the implications. For example, if your team is overloaded with Contributors, how has this affected team decision making, planning, problem solving, communication, and risk taking? On the other hand, if the team does not include the Contributor perspective, how has this adversely affected the operation of the team? Where possible, try to use actual examples from the team's recent history to assess the impact.

Table 9 includes two sample team profiles. All team members have completed the Team-Player Survey, and the location of the "X" indicates their primary team-player styles. In Sample Team Profile I, five of the eight team members are Contributors, and there are no Challengers on the team. What are the implications of their profile in terms of strengths and weaknesses? In other words, what do you suspect the team will do well, and where are their blind spots and potential weaknesses? If you know of such a team, can you cite

Table 9. Analyzing a Team Profile.

Sample Team Profile I: Contributor Overload/Challenger is missing.

Name/Style	Contributor	Collaborator	Communicator	Challenger
Glenn			X	
Dick		X		
Ira	X			
Peg	X			
David	X			
Maria	X			
Terry			X	
Judy	X			

Exercise: 1. Analyze the strengths and weaknesses of this team in terms of the following:

        a. planning
        b. communication
        c. risk taking
        d. problem solving
        e. decision making

     2. Recommend possible improvements.

Sample Team Profile II: Collaborator Overload/Communicator is missing.

Name/Style	Contributor	Collaborator	Communicator	Challenger
Jill		X		
Ellen	X			
Mike		X		
Alan		X		
Mindy		X		
Bill				X
Dave		X		
Don	X			

Exercise: 1. Analyze the strengths and weaknesses of the team in terms of the following:

        a. planning
        b. communication
        c. risk taking
        d. problem solving
        e. decision making

     2. Recommend possible improvements.

---

some team actions that reflect either the overload of task orientation or the absence of anyone willing to raise questions about the team?

In Sample Team Profile II, five of the eight team members are Collaborators, and there are no Communicators. What are the implications of this mix for the success of the team? Think of some teams that you believe may have this style composition. What do they do well? Where are they weak?

Chapter Eight

Developing a
Team-Player Culture

I strongly believe that people will exhibit behaviors that get recognized and rewarded.
—Bill McClung, Johnson & Johnson Baby Products*

In one way or another, most people in our survey believe that reward and recognition are the best ways to encourage effective team play. But differences arise in identifying the best method, and there is a gap between current approaches used by companies and those that are believed to work best. In our survey of major corporations, we asked people to indicate methods they currently use to create a team-player culture. We also asked for a list of recommended methods—approaches they have not yet tried but ones they believe will work. See Table 10 for a comparison.

Current Methods

Public Statements by Top Management. Teamwork is highly valued in organizations. Speeches at corporate meetings are filled with references to success being the result of "all of us pulling together." Upper-level management refers to the company "family" and the efforts of "all members of the team" in reaching the organization's goals. Many people sent me copies of company newspapers and annual reports that contained statements by corporate leaders acknowledging the importance of effective team players. It is important that public messages promote the value of team players and, at the time of award ceremonies, that such messages address the

*Survey response.

Table 10. Current and Recommended Methods of Developing
a Team-Player Culture.

Current	Recommended
1. Public Statements by Top Management	1. Promotion
2. Important Assignments	2. Upper Management as Team-Player Models
3. Training and Development	3. Performance Appraisal
4. Promotion	

specific contributions of individuals who are outstanding team players. The organization needs to hear from its leaders about the type of performance that is rewarded. As one of our survey respondents said, "We make it clear that good team play is expected and is necessary to meet our objectives."

Important Assignments. Since we know that team players like responsibility and a challenge, and to be part of something important, one current method of encouragement is to give team players important assignments. Some people see this as the best approach because it is a means to achieving better team players. If we can believe all of the so-called motivation-to-work survey results, then rewarding team players with better work opportunities makes great sense. One recent work-motivation study reported "opportunity to produce quality work (93%)" and "feeling that my work is important (89%)" at the top of a rank-order list of motivators (*Metrex Footnotes,* 1988, p. 3).

Training and Development. Many companies provide workshops in communication skills, meetings management, listening, assertiveness, conflict resolution, goal setting, and other topics that provide the skills necessary to be an effective team player. Some organizations also offer team-building consulting services to business teams and cross-functional groups. While these development opportunities send a message that the organization supports teamwork, it is not a strong message unless it is coupled with other corporate activities. In some companies, unfortunately, cynics see team workshops as "that touchy-feely stuff" produced by human resources.

Few sessions focus specifically on being a team player. Current workshops primarily address the effective team, the effective leader, or communication/leadership skills. More sessions are needed on the role of team player, increasing team-player effectiveness, and the dimensions of an effective team. It is not surprising that this kind of training was not selected by any of our survey respondents as a recommended motivator of team players. Clearly, while many companies offer workshops in this area, by itself, training is not perceived to be effective.

Recommended Strategies

Promotions. Many companies report that they promote people who are team players and are technically competent. This method overlaps the two categories—promotions are currently being used as a reward and they are recommended as a way of further motivating people to be more effective team players.

Floyd Whellan, vice-president of human resources at Lee Enterprises, says it directly: "We promote team players . . . [and] we make it clear that profit-goal accomplishment alone will not lead to promotion."

A promotion is a specific, visible reward, and it can be used both to reward team players and to send a message to others in the organization that team-player behaviors are valued. However, promotion by itself is not enough. The reasons for the promotion must be made clear and specific. When a person is promoted because he or she is both technically competent and an effective team player, the accomplishments in both areas should be highlighted. Here is an example of a short announcement:

Donna Jamieson
Promoted to Project Director

Donna Jamieson has been promoted to project director in recognition of her creativity as a systems developer on PBAT, YAM, and ORRIS. She continues to develop her technical skills via in-company workshops and external seminars, and she recently completed course requirements for an M.S. degree in computer science from S.U. As cochair of the user interface team and a member of the BIRKS Task Force, Donna has shown herself to be someone who can be depended upon to do her homework, to pitch in when other people need help, and to make sure everyone gets a chance to participate in team decisions. She is honest, ethical, and willing to speak her mind on important organizational issues. Donna contributes technical excellence as well as a positive team spirit to our organization.

It is important that everyone know that being an effective team player contributed to Donna's promotion. The promotion, including the text of the announcement, makes it clear that team players are valued and that getting ahead in this organization requires a demonstrated competence in technical and team-player skills.

One of the respondents to our survey went to the other end of the spectrum. He recommended the "removal from positions of authority managers who are not team players." Once again, when this type of action is contemplated, the positioning and the associated message must indicate that poor teamwork caused the removal.

Upper Management as Models of Effective Team Players. Many companies in our survey reported that the top leadership in their organizations talked about the importance of team players to the success of the enterprise. While statements about the need for teamwork are necessary, they are not sufficient. Our survey participants, including both top executives and midlevel managers, felt that "actions speak louder than words." And while that phrase may not mark a dramatic conceptual breakthrough, everyone agrees that, in organizations, people watch closely the behaviors of their leaders. In other words, they "read their lips" and watch their movements.

As a consultant, I have heard many managers complain about the lack of cooperation among the executive team. For example, a manager will see or hear about the executives' failure to work together. Occasionally, a manager will get an informal directive from his or her vice-president not to give information or in other ways not to help people in related organizations. In such cases, top management is not acting cooperatively and is discouraging its staff from practicing positive team play. Very quickly, people in the organization get the message—"We may talk about the value of teamwork, but we don't practice it." Clearly, however, positive modeling does work. When the leadership works as a team, being a team player becomes the organizational norm.

David Gilman, of Merrill Lynch, strongly emphasized the need for top management "actually emulating 'teamplayership' with their staff *and* encouraging them to assist others beyond their normal responsibility." And the former president of a major food company said, "It requires a strong message, in words and actions, from senior management."

Team Play as a Factor in Performance Appraisal. Once again, there is widespread agreement that those behaviors valued by the organization must be included in the performance appraisal process. While words like *teamwork* and *cooperation* are included in some appraisal forms, the meaning of these terms is not clear. If *team player* is incorporated as a performance factor, then the behaviors to be assessed should be specified. The list of behaviors outlined in Chapter Three would be a place to start. Several companies in our survey provided us with their appraisal forms, and those forms defined behaviors aligned with our view of team players.

Ameritech, the regional Bell operating company based in Chicago, assesses the following factors:

> Flexibility: Responsive to unscheduled requests. Able to shift tasks and maintain priorities. Adjusts to changing situations without undue stress or complaint.
> Innovativeness: Creatively develops new approaches to problems. Recommends efficiencies and new systems. Perceives and creates opportunities for improving job performance.
> Risk Taking: Decisive and willing to proceed without all available data. Appropriately operates outside of existing procedures.
> Teamwork: Effective as a team member. Constructively challenges prevailing points of view. Solicits supporting expertise as necessary.

Initiative and Drive: Self-starter. Seeks out opportunities to influence events. High energy level.

While Ameritech has *teamwork* as one of the performance factors, behaviors in all other categories are also associated with team players—most notably, the *risk-taking* actions we would associate with the Challenger, *flexibility* with the Collaborator, and *innovativeness* with the Contributor role. However, this form does not include the process behavior contributed by the Communicator.

Another company, Herman Miller Inc., does include the team-process behaviors of the Communicator in its appraisal form. Some of the team-player factors incorporated in their appraisal system are the following:

Relationships: Builds trust. Is friendly and approachable in working with others in and outside of work group.

Innovation: Solves problems creatively. Seeks, develops, and encourages new ideas.

Participation: Actively seeks the best solution by asking for ideas. Is open to unsolicited ideas and opinions. Offers ideas. Contributes actively as a team member. Inspires teamwork in others.

Accountability: Holds self responsible for understanding and meeting expectations. Takes initiative to identify and solve problems without blaming others.

Spirit: Is enthusiastic about work. Excites others through example.

These few examples demonstrate that it is possible to use the performance appraisal process as a strategy for encouraging people to be team players and, thereby, to establish teamwork as a corporate norm. More still can be done in this vein to support and develop team players.

Related to the appraisal process should be development planning. In many companies, each person has a development plan that indicates targeted future positions and activities designed to enhance the person's career development opportunities. Here is another place where team-player behavior can be reinforced. The development plan can emphasize the need for team-player behaviors and can include training, projects, and assignments designed to improve the needed skills and knowledge. In addition, the training workshops sponsored by the human resources department can be a useful supplement and support for the more powerful organizational development interventions.

Other Methods to Encourage and Reward Team Players

Awards. Team recognition through awards is a controversial suggestion. Some companies include team awards in the corporate awards program. They firmly believe such awards promote teamwork by recognizing the efforts of specific work groups or task forces. These awards usually involve cash payments plus other items such as plaques, team pictures, and stories in the company newspapers.

Opponents argue that award programs are divisive. They believe that people who do not get awards can turn sour and unproductive and that the net result is discouragement. Only "hot" projects are recognized, and in the opponents' view, many people are on teams that are just "toiling in the vineyards"—performing the basic work of the company—and have no chance for an award. The opponents of team awards see politics influencing the decisions and believe that upper management cannot clearly see the good work done by teams.

One possible answer to this objection is the Peer Recognition Awards Program devised by General Electric's Space Systems Division in Philadelphia. Here an employee peer review board develops the award guidelines, reviews all proposals, makes the decisions, and announces the awards.

Salary Increases. Tangible rewards do not have to come in the form of an award or cash bonus. Salary treatment is another approach. If the appraisal system and development planning use the team-player behaviors in their decision making, it makes sense to give higher merit increases and salary adjustments to employees who perform well in both job task accomplishment and team-player skills. And, once again, the employee should be told the reason for the salary decision as a way of reinforcing the appropriate behaviors.

Incentive Plans. Most incentive plans tied to company profits are geared to individual bonuses. They do not encourage teamwork and in some cases actually result in an increase in selfish behavior. Sauer (1989) has devised a plan that is tied to company profits and that rewards team effort. This is not for everyone. The plan requires an organization in which there is (1) a high level of trust among team members, (2) a willingness to disclose financial information to team members, (3) a team approach to getting the work done, and (4) good communication to the teams about the program.

Briefly, the plan requires the identification of teams for inclusion, a target incentive for each team (usually a percentage of the salary grade midpoint), and then tying each target level "to a specific percentile performance of return on assets that must be exceeded to receive that incentive reward" (Sauer, 1989, p. 40).

The Scanlon Plan is an employee incentive program with a heavy dose of participation. Scanlon and other similar plans, such as Rucker and Improshare, all pay employees bonuses based on some formula associated with productivity gains or cost savings. These incentive programs have come to be known as *gainsharing* (Lawler, 1986, pp. 144–169). Thus far, gainsharing has not extended far beyond manufacturing environments. Gainsharing results should be studied by organization-development and compensation specialists as a basis for devising incentive systems for employees in other work areas.

Compensation Systems. As we discussed in Chapter One, even selling, that most individualistic of occupations, is moving to a team approach. With many salespeople working on a single account, compensation must support and encourage teamwork and ensure fair treatment for each person. Cespedes, Doyle, and Freedman (1989), who studied four companies with sizable sales forces, argue for flexibility in compensation systems, with different approaches for different types of accounts. For example, "If there are many salespeople calling on key accounts and teamwork is important, then a bonus based on total account sales often makes more sense than traditional, individually oriented incentive arrangements" (p. 46). Another problem is with large accounts. Teamwork is usually required, and closing the sales can take months, even years. And since most compensation systems are geared to short-term results, salespeople are not encouraged to work as a team on these large accounts. However, Cespedes, Doyle, and Freedman point out that "bonuses for multi-year performance, or for qualitative objectives like building relationships with certain account decision-makers, can encourage team effort" (p. 46).

Management Assessment Program. Some companies include teamwork as a competency factor in their assessment center programs. Anheuser-Busch, for example, incorporates team-related competencies (for example, group management) as part of its management competency model. If the assessment program is aimed at identifying people for leadership positions in the company, then team-player skills should be measured along with such competencies as problem solving, creativity, and communication.

Team Recognition. There are many nonmonetary forms of reward that encourage and support team-player behaviors. By the way, all of this discussion assumes that people in the organization perceive the financial rewards to be adequate and fair. No form of recognition will work unless the basic needs are being addressed.

Technical and scientific personnel are often the least interested in teamwork. They enjoy working alone and are rewarded for their individual achievements. And yet, as Mower and Wilemon (1989) have shown, technical professionals will work together when there is thoughtful recognition for their efforts and, especially, when there is respect from their peers. Mower and Wilemon (p. 25) cite these examples of team recognition:

- Publicity in newspapers, company publications and other corporate media
- Commendation at a company gathering
- Plaques and certificates
- Gifts/Honorific titles
- A night "on the town"

- A trip to a conference
- Dinner with the CEO
- Vacation with spouse
- Journal subscription
- Grants to charities of the team's choosing
- Scholarships in the team's name

These forms of recognition tend to appeal to extrinsic motivation; they are external rewards. However, extrinsic rewards (1) can be overused to the point where they lose value, (2) are seen by some recipients as manipulative, and (3) are just not effective with people who are turned off by external recognition. Many technical professionals and others are more motivated by internal rewards such as challenging work, increased responsibility, and an opportunity to learn. In an effort to appeal to intrinsic motivation, Mower and Wilemon (p. 26) suggest the following forms of team recognition:

- Being asked to take on difficult tasks
- Increasing scope of team assignments
- Increasing variety of work
- Seeking team advice on problems
- Top Managers being interested, paying visits
- Increased freedom and flexibility
- Use of team outputs
- Using the team as consultants to other teams
- "Leadership" shared by team members
- Opportunity to master new technology
- A professionally stimulating environment

Team recognition only works as a supporter of team-player behaviors when the mission of the team requires real task interdependence. In other words, the work can be completed satisfactorily only if members share expertise, set joint goals, regularly interact, and are willing to raise questions and challenge each other. Some teams are really not teams but groups of people tied together by what we referred to earlier as administrative convenience. These groups are teams in name only because the work is a series of discrete tasks that do not require any coordination.

When real teamwork is required, recognition can be a powerful motivator for effective team players. And most important from an organizational standpoint, "Teams rewarded on a strictly team basis, with everybody sharing equally, almost always outperform teams in which certain persons are rewarded more than others" (Mower and Wilemon, 1989, pp. 27-28).

Eliminate Competitive Rating Systems. Rating and ranking systems that pit employees against each other in the annual performance review process tend to work against the development of teamwork. A ranking system that includes a requirement for a bell-shaped-curve distribution further emphasizes competition over cooperation.

Under this system, employees know that in the final analysis, their performance will be compared with other employees—even those on the same work team. This fact alone impacts their willingness to be effective team players. Many employees have told me that they are reluctant to share technical expertise because it may help another person obtain a better rating and a higher rank. "Why should I be a team player when my appraisal is based solely on my individual contribution?" is the question asked by many employees.

Two employees who had to work together throughout the year and enjoyed being team players tried an experiment. During the year, all of their work (reports, programs, and memos) was published under joint authorship. They accomplished a great deal and were satisfied with their effort as a team. However, in preparation for the annual division appraisal meeting, their manager asked that they indicate specifically who prepared each document. The system required that there be some way of differentiating them!

R_x for the Development of a Team-Player Culture

1. Public statements by corporate leaders on the importance of team players—not just the importance of teamwork.
2. Executives and senior managers serving as models of team players.
3. Promoting people who are both technically competent and team players with appropriate public announcements that

      emphasize team-player skills as an important factor in the promotions.

4. Giving important assignments to positive team players.
5. Incorporating team-player behaviors in the performance appraisal system.
6. Training workshops on the skills of an effective team player.
7. Giving higher salary increases to positive team players.
8. Developing incentive systems that reward team effort.
9. Designing flexible compensation programs that pay individuals for their contributions to a team approach.
10. Including team-player competencies in the management assessment process.
11. Developing a program of team awards that are tailored to the motivational needs of the organization.
12. Encouraging managers to use a variety of nonmonetary forms of recognition that appeal to intrinsic motivation.
13. Eliminating competitive rating and ranking performance appraisal systems that do not value team-player contributions.

Chapter Nine

Challenges for
Teams and Team Players

Teamwork does not happen by accident. People are not born to be team players. As Alfie Kohn (1986) has shown, Americans are trained to be competitive rather than cooperative. Organizations that adopt teamwork as a strategy for success must develop plans for meeting the challenges at various levels of the organization.

The Executive Challenge

Leaders at the top of the house must be prepared to say the right words and then to make them come alive on a daily basis. Many organizations adopt a vision statement or a list of corporate values. These statements usually call for teamwork, quality, customer service, and other admirable goals. Copies of the statements are found in company publications and are usually displayed in prominent company locations. Statements are necessary but not sufficient. Executives who want team play to be a way of life must examine every important decision in light of its impact on that concept. Visitors at the corporate offices of Hoechst-Celanese Corporation in Somerville, New Jersey, find a framed copy of the Corporate Values on the wall of every office and conference room. The Hoechst-Celanese values include teamwork throughout the organization; participative goal setting, measurement, and feedback; and decision making at the lowest level.

Visitors are also told that Ernest H. Drew, CEO of Hoechst-Celanese, measures each executive decision for its consistency with both the spirit and content of the values. All executives and managers throughout the organization are expected to do the same.

The Management Challenge

Managers must act in ways that support team players. When task forces, committees, and business teams are formed, managers should look for diversity of team-player styles in selecting team members. When performance appraisals, salary reviews, and promotion decisions are made, team-player accomplishments must be weighed equally with task accomplishments. And when rewards and recognition are distributed, team players should be acknowledged in ways that demonstrate the importance of teamwork to the success of the organization.

The Human Resources Challenge

Human resources professionals must incorporate the team-player concept in all policies and procedures. Recruitment and hiring literature and procedures should make it clear that the organization values team players. In other words, "Solo operators need not apply." Interview questions and reference checks should look for team-player characteristics, and the performance appraisal process should be revised to include the team-player behaviors. Similarly, the team-player characteristics should be added to the competencies in the organization's management assessment program.

The Training and Development Challenge

Training professionals must include workshops designed to foster team-player skills and effective teamwork. The first step is a basic program in the team-player styles and the characteristics of an effective team. In this workshop, participants learn to identify their team-player styles and to increase their personal effectiveness. The workshop should also provide a framework to assess their current team against the twelve characteristics of an effective team and to develop a plan for improvement.

The basic workshop should be the gateway to successive modules focusing on specific team-player skills:

- Planning and goal setting
- Meetings management
- Listening
- Resolving conflict
- Consensus building
- Presentations
- Risk taking
- Problem solving
- Role clarification
- Mentorship
- Ethics
- Assertiveness
- Feedback
- Monitoring and evaluation
- Dealing with ineffective team players
- Rewards and recognition

The training challenge is growing as jobs are requiring greater skills and as the public school system is not meeting companies' needs in basic reading and math. The challenge goes beyond literacy training to include reasoning, following instructions, and working in teams; many companies are using self-managing work teams, quality circles, and other employee involvement methods.

The Personal Challenge

For you, the challenge is to be the best possible team player. This means many things:

1. Know your style, including the strengths and the potential for ineffectiveness.
2. Develop a plan to optimize your strengths and minimize your shortcomings.

3. Look for ways to expand your repertoire by increasing the use of the behaviors of other team-player styles.

4. Be aware of your team's stage of development and the needs associated with that stage. Provide your team with the team-player assistance required, and encourage others to do the same.

5. Acknowledge that other members of your team will have different styles. Be willing to work with others with different styles and to see this diversity as a team strength.

6. As a team leader, know the twelve dimensions of an effective team, assess your team's effectiveness, build on your strengths, and plan to reduce your weaknesses.

7. Persist and persevere. Teamwork is work.

8. And smile, you're having fun!

═══════ Resources ═══════

Tools for Developing
Teams and Team Players

A. Team-Development Survey

B. Team-Development Survey: Summary
and Action-Planning Guide

C. Team-Player Survey

D. Team-Player Styles

Note: For information on obtaining the Team-Development Survey and the Team-Player Survey, please contact Glenn M. Parker Associates, 795 Parkway Avenue, Trenton, New Jersey 08618.

Team-Development Survey

How Often Is This Statement True?

(Circle one number)

Statements	Seldom	Sometimes	Often	Very Frequently
1. *Clear Purpose:* The vision, mission, goal, or task of the team has been defined and is accepted by everyone. There is an action plan. Comments: _____	1 2	3 4	5 6	7 8
2. *Informality:* The climate tends to be informal, comfortable, and relaxed. There are no obvious tensions or signs of boredom. Comments: _____	1 2	3 4	5 6	7 8
3. *Participation:* There is a lot of discussion, and everyone is encouraged to participate. Comments: _____	1 2	3 4	5 6	7 8
4. *Listening:* The members use effective listening techniques such as questioning, paraphrasing, and summarizing to get out ideas. Comments: _____	1 2	3 4	5 6	7 8
5. *Civilized Disagreement:* There is disagreement, but the team is comfortable with this and shows no signs of avoiding, smoothing over, or suppressing conflict. Comments: _____	1 2	3 4	5 6	7 8

		Statements	*Seldom*	*Sometimes*	*Often*	*Very Frequently*

6. *Consensus Decisions:* For important decisions, the goal is substantial but not necessarily unanimous agreement through open discussion of everyone's ideas and avoidance of formal voting and easy compromises.
   Comments: _____
   _____

   1 2   3 4   5 6   7 8

7. *Open Communication:* Team members feel free to express their feelings on the task as well as on the group's operation. There are few hidden agendas. Communication takes place outside of meetings.
   Comments: _____
   _____

   1 2   3 4   5 6   7 8

8. *Clear Roles and Work Assignments:* There are clear expectations about the roles played by each team member. When action is taken, clear assignments are made, accepted, and carried out. Work is fairly distributed among team members.
   Comments: _____
   _____

   1 2   3 4   5 6   7 8

9. *Shared Leadership:* While the team has a formal leader, leadership functions shift from time to time depending upon the circumstances, the needs of the group, and the skills of the members. The formal leader models the appropriate behavior and helps establish positive norms.
   Comments: _____
   _____

   1 2   3 4   5 6   7 8

10. *External Relations:* The team spends time developing key outside relationships, mobilizing re-

Statements	Seldom	Sometimes	Often	Very Frequently

sources, and building credibility with important players in other parts of the organization.
    1 2   3 4   5 6   7 8
Comments: _____

11. *Style Diversity:* The team has a broad spectrum of team-player types including members who emphasize attention to tasks, goal setting, a focus on process, and questions about how the team is functioning.
    1 2   3 4   5 6   7 8
Comments: _____

12. *Self-Assessment:* Periodically, the team stops to examine how well it is functioning and what may be interfering with its effectiveness.
    1 2   3 4   5 6   7 8
Comments: _____

Team-Development Survey: Summary and Action-Planning Guide

1. What are the strengths of your team?

2. In what areas do you need to improve?

3. Identify action steps to improve the functioning of your team.

Team-Player Survey

Purpose

The Team-Player Survey will help you identify your style as a team player. The results will lead you to an assessment of your current strengths and provide a basis for a plan to increase your effectiveness as a team player.

Teams may use the survey to develop a profile of team strengths and to discuss strategies for increasing team effectiveness.

Directions

First, this is a survey, and, therefore, there are no right or wrong answers. Please answer each item according to how you honestly feel you function now as a team member rather than how you used to be or how you would like to be.

You will be asked to complete eighteen sentences. Each sentence has four possible endings. Please rank the endings in the order in which you feel each one applies to you. Place the number 4 next to the ending which is most applicable to you and continue down to a 1 next to the ending which is least applicable to you.

For example:

As a team member, I am usually most concerned about:
_____ a. meeting high ethical standards.
_____ b. reaching our goals.
_____ c. meeting my individual responsibilities.
_____ d. how well we are working together as a group.

Please do not make ties or use 4, 3, 2, or 1 more than once. It is possible that some of the sentences will have two or more endings that apply to you or will have none that applies to you, but you should assume these are your only choices and rank them accordingly. Each set of endings must be ranked 4, 3, 2, and 1.

THE TEAM-PLAYER SURVEY

1. During team meetings, I usually:
   _____ a. provide the team with technical data or information.
   _____ b. keep the team focused on our mission or goals.
   _____ c. make sure everyone is involved in the discussion.
   _____ d. raise questions about our goals or methods.

2. In relating to the team leader, I:
   _____ a. suggest that our work be goal directed.
   _____ b. try to help him or her build a positive team climate.
   _____ c. am willing to disagree with him or her when necessary.
   _____ d. offer advice based upon my area of expertise.

3. Under stress, I sometimes:
   _____ a. overuse humor and other tension-reducing devices.
   _____ b. am too direct in communicating with other team members.
   _____ c. lose patience with the need to get everyone involved in
             discussions.
   _____ d. complain to outsiders about problems facing the team.

4. When conflicts arise on the team, I usually:
   _____ a. press for an honest discussion of the differences.
   _____ b. provide reasons why one side or the other is correct.
   _____ c. see the differences as a basis for a possible change in team
             direction.
   _____ d. try to break the tension with a supportive or humorous
             remark.

5. Other team members usually see me as:
   _____ a. factual.
   _____ b. flexible.
   _____ c. encouraging.
   _____ d. candid.

6. At times, I am:
   _____ a. too results oriented.
   _____ b. too laid-back.
   _____ c. self-righteous.
   _____ d. shortsighted.

7. When things go wrong on the team, I usually:
   _____ a. push for increased emphasis on listening, feedback, and
             participation.
   _____ b. press for a candid discussion of our problems.
   _____ c. work hard to provide more and better information.
   _____ d. suggest that we revisit our basic mission.

8. A risky team contribution for me is to:
_____ a. question some aspect of the team's work.
_____ b. push the team to set higher performance standards.
_____ c. work outside my defined role or job area.
_____ d. provide other team members with feedback on their behavior as team members.

9. Sometimes other team members see me as:
_____ a. a perfectionist.
_____ b. unwilling to reassess the team's mission or goals.
_____ c. not serious about getting the real job done.
_____ d. a nitpicker.

10. I believe team problem solving requires:
_____ a. cooperation by all team members.
_____ b. high-level listening skills.
_____ c. a willingness to ask tough questions.
_____ d. good solid data.

11. When a new team is forming, I usually:
_____ a. try to meet and get to know other team members.
_____ b. ask pointed questions about our goals and methods.
_____ c. want to know what is expected of me.
_____ d. seek clarity about our basic mission.

12. At times, I make other people feel:
_____ a. dishonest because they are not able to be as confrontational as I am.
_____ b. guilty because they don't live up to my standards.
_____ c. small-minded because they don't think long-range.
_____ d. heartless because they don't care about how people relate to each other.

13. I believe the role of the team leader is to:
_____ a. ensure the efficient solution of business problems.
_____ b. help the team establish long-range goals and short-term objectives.
_____ c. create a participatory decision-making climate.
_____ d. bring out diverse ideas and challenge assumptions.

14. I believe team decisions should be based on:
_____ a. the team's mission and goals.
_____ b. a consensus of team members.
_____ c. an open and candid assessment of the issues.
_____ d. the weight of the evidence.

15. Sometimes I:
_____ a. see team climate as an end in itself.
_____ b. play devil's advocate far too long.

_____ c. fail to see the importance of effective team process.

_____ d. overemphasize strategic issues and minimize short-term task accomplishments.

16. People have often described me as:

_____ a. independent.

_____ b. dependable.

_____ c. imaginative.

_____ d. participative.

17. Most of the time, I am:

_____ a. responsible and hardworking.

_____ b. committed and flexible.

_____ c. enthusiastic and humorous.

_____ d. honest and authentic.

18. In relating to other team members, at times I get annoyed because they don't:

_____ a. revisit team goals to check progress.

_____ b. see the importance of working well together.

_____ c. object to team actions with which they disagree.

_____ d. complete their team assignments on time.

TEAM-PLAYER SURVEY RESULTS

Directions:
1. Please transfer your answers from the survey to this page.
2. Please be careful when recording the numbers because the order of the letters changes for each questions. For example, in question #1, the order is a, b, c, d, but in question #2, the order is d, a, b, c.
3. The totals for the four styles must equal 180.

Question	Contributor	Collaborator	Communicator	Challenger
1.	a. _____	b. _____	c. _____	d. _____
2.	d. _____	a. _____	b. _____	c. _____
3.	c. _____	d. _____	a. _____	b. _____
4.	b. _____	c. _____	d. _____	a. _____
5.	a. _____	b. _____	c. _____	d. _____
6.	d. _____	a. _____	b. _____	c. _____
7.	c. _____	d. _____	a. _____	b. _____
8.	b. _____	c. _____	d. _____	a. _____
9.	a. _____	b. _____	c. _____	d. _____
10.	d. _____	a. _____	b. _____	c. _____
11.	c. _____	d. _____	a. _____	b. _____
12.	b. _____	c. _____	d. _____	a. _____
13.	a. _____	b. _____	c. _____	d. _____
14.	d. _____	a. _____	b. _____	c. _____
15.	c. _____	d. _____	a. _____	b. _____
16.	b. _____	c. _____	d. _____	a. _____
17.	a. _____	b. _____	c. _____	d. _____
18.	d. _____	a. _____	b. _____	c. _____
TOTALS	_____	_____	_____	_____ = 180

The highest number designates your primary team-player style. If your highest numbers are the same or within three points of each other, consider them both as your primary style. The lowest total indicates your least active team-player style.

Your primary team-player style defines a set of behaviors that you use most often as a member of a team. It does not mean that it is the only style you use. All of us have the capacity to use any one of the four styles. We simply use one style—our primary style—most often.

Team-Player Styles

Contributor   *Task*

The Contributor is a task-oriented team member who enjoys providing the team with good technical information and data, does his or her homework, and pushes the team to set high performance standards and to use their resources wisely. Most people see you as dependable, although they believe, at times, that you may become too bogged down in the details and data or that you do not see the big picture or the need for positive team climate.

People describe you as responsible, authoritative, reliable, proficient, and organized.

Collaborator   *Goal*

The Collaborator is a goal-directed member who sees the vision, mission, or goal of the team as paramount but is flexible and open to new ideas, willing to pitch in and work outside his or her defined role, and able to share the limelight with other team members. Most people see you as a big-picture person, but they believe, at times, that you may fail periodically to revisit the mission, to give enough attention to the basic team tasks, or to consider the individual needs of other team members.

People describe you as forward-looking, goal directed, accommodating, flexible, and imaginative.

Communicator   *Process*

The Communicator is a process-oriented member who is an effective listener and facilitator of involvement, conflict resolution, consensus building, feedback, and the building of an informal, relaxed climate. Most people see you as a positive "people person, " but they find that, at times, you may see process as an end in itself, may not confront other team members, or may not give enough emphasis to completing task assignments and making progress toward team goals.

People describe you as supportive, considerate, relaxed, enthusiastic, and tactful.

Challenger   *Question*

The Challenger is a member who questions the goals, methods, and even the ethics of the team, is willing to disagree with the leader or higher authority, and encourages the team to take well-conceived risks. Most people appreciate the value of your candor and openness, but they think, at times, that you may not know when to back off an issue or that you become self-righteous and try to push the team too far.

People describe you as honest, outspoken, principled, ethical, and adventurous.

References

Alster, N. "What Flexible Workers Can Do." *Fortune*, Feb. 13, 1989, pp. 62–66.

Argyris, C. *Integrating the Individual and the Organization.* New York: Wiley, 1964.

Atkins, S. *The Name of Your Game.* Beverly Hills, Calif.: Ellis & Stewart, 1981.

Barmore, G. T. "Teamwork: Charting a Course for Success." *Mortgage Banking*, Aug. 1987, pp. 92–96.

Beckard, R. "ABS in Health Care Systems." *Journal of Applied Behavioral Science*, 1974, *10* (1), 93–106.

Bennis, W. G. Speech presented at Best of America Human Resources Conference sponsored by *Training Magazine* and *Personnel Journal*, New York, Dec. 12, 1988.

Bennis, W. G. *Why Leaders Can't Lead: The Unconscious Conspiracy Continues.* San Francisco: Jossey-Bass, 1989.

Bennis, W. G., and Nanus, B. *Leaders: The Strategies for Taking Charge.* New York: Harper & Row, 1985.

Bennis, W. G., and Slater, P. *The Temporary Society.* New York: Harper & Row, 1968.

Berger, J. "Companies Step In Where the Schools Fail." *New York Times*, Sept. 26, 1989, pp. 158–170.

Blake, R., and Mouton, J. S. *The Managerial Grid.* Houston, Tex.: Gulf, 1964.

Blake, R., and Mouton, J. S. *Building a Dynamic Corporation Through Grid Organization Development.* Reading, Mass.: Addison-Wesley, 1969.

Block, P. *The Empowered Manager: Positive Political Skills at Work.* San Francisco: Jossey-Bass, 1987.

Bradford, D., and Cohen, A. R. *Managing for Excellence.* New York: Wiley, 1984.

Briggs, K. C., and Myers, I. B. *Myers-Briggs Type Indicator (F).* Princeton, N.J.: Educational Testing Service, 1957.

Cespedes, F. V., Doyle, S. X., and Freedman, R. J. "Teamwork for Today's Selling." *Harvard Business Review,* Mar.-Apr. 1989, pp. 44-48.

Chance, P. "Great Experiments in Team Chemistry." *Across the Board,* May 1989, pp. 18-24.

Chubb, J. E. "Why the Current Wave of School Reform Will Fail." *The Public Interest,* Winter 1988, pp. 28-49.

Cohen, S. S. "Beyond Macho: The Power of Womanly Management." *Working Woman,* Feb. 1989, pp. 77-83.

Coleman, D. "Psychologists Find Ways to Break Racism's Hold." *New York Times,* Sept. 5, 1989, pp. C1, C8.

"Copy Cats Worth Copying." *Management Solutions,* Jan. 1988, p. 28.

Crosby, P. *Quality Is Free.* New York: New American Library, 1979.

Dayal, I., and Thomas, J. M. "Operation KPE: Developing a New Organization." *Journal of Applied Behavioral Science,* 1968, *4* (4), 473-506.

Dionne, J. L. "The Art of Acquisitions." *Journal of Business Strategy,* Nov.-Dec. 1988, *9,* 12-18.

Dowst, S., and Raia, E. "Design '88: Teaming Up." *Purchasing,* Mar. 10, 1988, pp. 80-90.

Dumaine, B. "How Managers Can Succeed Through Speed." *Fortune,* Feb. 3, 1989a, pp. 54-59.

Dumaine, B. "P&G Rewrites the Marketing Rules." *Fortune,* Nov. 6, 1989b, pp. 35-48.

Dyer, W. G. *Team Building: Issues and Alternatives.* Reading, Mass.: Addison-Wesley, 1987.

Epstein, D. "The Team Approach." *Restaurant Business,* Jan. 20, 1989, p. 48.

"Ethical Values and Principles." *Ethics: Easier Said Than Done,* Spring/Summer 1988, p. 153.

Evans, W. H., and Baker, J. L., Jr. "Drafting the World Series Team." *Mortgage Banking,* June 1987, pp. 40–47.

Feder, R., and Mitchell, J. "4-day Task Force More Efficient Than Traditional Problem-Solving." *Marketing News,* Aug. 29, 1988, p. 21.

Franke, J. J., Jr. "Innovation and Teamwork." *The Bureaucrat,* Winter 1988–89, pp. 11–12.

Golembiewski, R., and Eddy, W. *Organization Development in Public Administration.* New York: Marcel Dekker, 1978.

Goslin, R. "Eight Steps to Applications Engineering." *Datamation,* Nov. 1, 1988, pp. 59–62.

Harrison, R. "Role Negotiations." In W. Burke and H. Hornstein (eds.), *The Social Technology of Organization Development.* Washington, D.C.: NTL Learning Resources, 1971.

Hart, L. B. *Learning from Conflict.* Reading, Mass.: Addison-Wesley, 1980.

Harvey, J. "The Abilene Paradox: The Management of Agreement." *Organizational Dynamics,* Summer 1974, pp. 17–34.

Hastings, C., Bixby, P., and Chaudhry-Lawton, R. *The Superteam Solution.* San Diego, Calif.: University Associates, 1987.

Herman, S. M., and Herman, M. D. "Special Teams, Properly Used, Can Create Effective Solutions." *Personnel Administrator,* Oct. 1989, pp. 90–92.

Jackall, R. "Moral Mazes: Bureaucracy and Managerial Work." *Harvard Business Review,* Sept.–Oct. 1983, pp. 118–130.

Jamieson, D. W., and O'Mara, J. *Flex-Management: Managing the Changing Workforce* (tentative). San Francisco: Jossey-Bass, forthcoming.

Janus, I. *Victims of Groupthink.* Boston: Houghton Mifflin, 1972.

Jung, C. G. *Psychological Types.* New York: Pantheon Books, 1923.

Kanter, R. M. *The Change Masters.* New York: Simon & Schuster, 1983.

Kapstein, J., and Hoerr, J. "Volvo's Radical New Plant: The Death of the Assembly Line?" *Business Week,* Aug. 28, 1989, pp. 92–93.

Kertesz, L. "Team Concept Makes Mazda Flat Rock a Different Plant." *Automotive News,* Feb. 29, 1988, p. 36.

Kohn, A. *No Contest.* Boston: Houghton Mifflin, 1986.

Kouzes, J. M., and Posner, B. Z. *The Leadership Challenge: How to Get Extraordinary Things Done in Organizations.* San Francisco: Jossey-Bass, 1987.

Kull, D. "Software Development: The Consensus Approach." *Computer and Communications Decisions,* Aug. 1987, pp. 63–69.

Lambert, L. "The End of the Era of Staff Development." *Educational Leadership,* 1989, 7 (1), 79–81.

Larson, C. "Team Tactics Can Cut Product Development Costs." *Journal of Business Strategy,* Sept.–Oct. 1988, *9,* 22–25.

Lawler, E. E., III. *High-Involvement Management: Participative Strategies for Improving Organizational Performance.* San Francisco: Jossey-Bass, 1986.

Leavitt, D. "Team Techniques in System Development." *Datamation,* Nov. 15, 1987, pp. 78–86.

Lee, B. "Worker Harmony Makes NUMMI Work." *New York Times,* Dec. 25, 1988, Sec. 3, p. 2.

Lewin, K. *Field Theory in Social Science.* New York: Harper & Row, 1951.

Likert, R. *New Patterns of Management.* New York: McGraw-Hill, 1961.

McGregor, D. M. *The Human Side of Enterprise.* New York: McGraw-Hill, 1960.

Merchant, J. E. "Teamwork for Profit." *Credit and Financial Management,* May 1987, pp. 33–34.

Metrex Footnotes. Newsletter. Tryon, N.C.: Metrex, Dec. 1988.

Moore, P. D. "New Ways to Reach Your Customers." *Fortune,* Nov. 6, 1989, p. 210.

Mower, J. C., and Wilemon, D. "Rewarding Technical Teamwork." *Research-Technology Management,* Sept.–Oct. 1989, pp. 24–29.

Pennar, K., and Mandel, M. "Economic Prospects for the Year 2000." *Business Week,* Sept. 25, 1989, pp. 158–170.

Peters, T. *Thriving on Chaos.* New York: Knopf, 1987.

Pugh, D. S., and Hickson, D. J. *Writers on Organizations.* Beverly Hills, Calif.: Sage, 1989.

Rowe, A. J., and Mason, R. O. *Managing with Style: A Guide to Understanding, Assessing, and Improving Decision Making.* San Francisco: Jossey-Bass, 1987.

Sauer, R. L. "For Managers and Stockholders: Win-Win Incentives." *Compensation and Benefits Review,* Mar.–Apr. 1989, pp. 38–45.

Schmuck, R. A., Runkel, P. L., and Langmeier, D. "Improving Organizational Problem-Solving in a School Facility." *Journal of Applied Behavioral Science,* 1969, *5* (4), 455–483.

Traub, J. "Into the Mouths of Babes." *New York Times Magazine,* July 24, 1988, pp. 18–53.

Tuckman, B. W. "Developmental Sequence in Small Groups." *Psychological Bulletin,* 1965, *63* (6), 384–399.

Versical, D. "Maker-Labor-Supplier Teamwork Urged for Industry." *Automotive News,* Aug. 10, 1987, p. 22.

Walton, R. *Interpersonal Peacemaking: Confrontation and Third Party Consultation.* Reading, Mass.: Addison-Wesley, 1969.

Weinstein, S. "Tyranny Is Out, Teamwork Is In." *Progressive Grocer,* Dec. 1987, pp. 150–156.

Wolff, M. F. "Teams Speed Commercialization of R & D Projects." *Research-Technology Management,* Sept.–Oct. 1988, pp. 8–10.

Index

The **Jossey-Bass Management Series** is about people committed to promoting responsible change. With our books, audios, and periodicals, we offer "The Best of the Best" in management thought—the essential tools for charting a clear and thoughtful course to becoming better agents of responsible change in a world that begs each of us for effective and continuous leadership.

Additional Management Insights from Jossey-Bass Publishers

		Price	x Qty	= Total

The Definitive Guide to Building a Team Approach

1-55542-609-3 Cross-Functional Teams: Working with Allies, Enemies, and Other Strangers
by Glenn M. Parker

$24.00 x _____ = _____

0-7879-0057-5 Who's Got the Ball? (and Other Nagging Questions About Team Life) A Player's Guide for Work Teams
by Coach Maureen O'Brien

$22.00 x _____ = _____

1-55542-638-7 The Skilled Facilitator: Practical Wisdom for Developing Effective Groups
by Roger M. Schwarz

$29.95 x _____ = _____

1-55542-613-1 Leadership Trapeze: Strategies for Leadership in Team-Based Organizations
by Jeanne M. Wilson, Jill George, Richard S. Wellins, with William C. Byham

$25.00 x _____ = _____

MAIL
✖ USE THIS ORDER FORM

FAX
800.605.BOOK (2665)
TOLL FREE 24 HOURS A DAY

Available at fine bookstores, or order direct:

Please send me the titles I have indicated above. I am enclosing $_____ , including shipping and appropriate state sales tax. (All payments must be prepaid, in U.S. dollars only.)

❏ check/money order ❏ Visa
❏ Mastercard ❏ American Express

Card no.: _____

Exp. date_____Day telephone _____

Signature_____

Shipping Charges for Prepaid Orders: $10 and under, add $2.50; $10.01-$20, add $3.50; $20.01-$50, add $4.50; $50.01-$75, add $5.50. CA, NJ, Washington, D.C., and NY residents add sales tax. Canadian residents add GST. Prices and availability subject to change without notice. Valid in the U.S. and Canada only.

Name _____

Address _____

City_____ State _____Zip_____

Jossey-Bass Publishers • 350 Sansome Street • San Francisco, CA 94104